Guide

ISBN 0-88813-005-8

Copyright: 1977
National Library of Canada
Ottawa

Quebec National Library
Montreal

The Montreal Museum of Fine Arts

Preface 4

As you visit the galleries, this guide will serve as an aid to your understanding the nature of the displays, the history of the collections, the selection of new acquisitions and the unique quality of particular exhibits.

The history of the Museum begins in the year 1847 with the birth of the Montreal Society of Artists, the precursor of the Art Association of Montreal established in 1860. As a result of reincorporation in 1948-49, the Association changed its name to the Montreal Museum of Fine Arts. In 1972, the institution became a semi-public corporation. The first home of the Art Association was a building on Phillips Square completed in 1879. In 1912 the Art Association moved to the Museum's present location on Sherbrooke Street. The Neo-classical building was designed by Edward and W. S. Maxwell. On May 8, 1976, the new wing designed by Fred Lebensold was officially inaugurated.

The first sizable donation of pictures to the Museum's collection was made by Benaiah Gibb in 1879. This bequest coincides with the Museum's first purchase of an Old Master painting, *Woman at the Harpsichord* attributed to Emanuel de Witte. By far the largest part of the picture collection has been left to the Museum by industrialists and railroad and shipping merchants. Today the Museum's collection encompasses works of international as well as Canadian provenance and includes a variety of artistic media.

The principle of including decorative arts in the collections was instigated in 1916 through the efforts and donations of Mr. F. Cleveland Morgan. The collection of decorative arts was further enriched in 1944 by an extensive bequest of oriental ceramics from the estate of Miss Adaline Van Horne. The Lucile Pillow collection of English porcelain and the Père Ernest Gagnon collection of African and Oceanic art are the latest massive donations in this domain.

This guide to the Museum was written to commemorate the opening of the new wing of the Museum. It represents the fruit of significant research, cataloguing, selection, and interpretation of the works of art in the collection which was undertaken by the curators for the new installation of the Museum. Funds for part of this cataloguing project were donated by National Museums Canada.

Under the direction of Dr. Myra Nan Rosenfeld, Research Curator, the following staff members have contributed to the preparation of this guide:

Miss Janet M. Brooke
    Assistant Curator
Mr. Jacques Dumouchel
    Assistant Curator
Miss Claudette Hould
    Assistant Curator
Mr. Germain Lefebvre
    Associate Curator,
    Canadian Art
Dr. Yakata Mino
    Associate Curator,
    Asiatic Art
Dr. Micheline Moisan
    Associate Curator,
    Prints and Drawings
Dr. Hayat Salam-Liebich
    Associate Curator,
    Islamic Art
Mrs. Joan Thornley
    Assistant to the Research
    Curator

The guide was translated by Mrs. Camille Letourneau and Mrs. Effat Bassal. Most of the photographs were taken by Lynton Gardiner.

David G. Carter, Director.

This guide is a complement to the didactic panels and labels in the galleries. The didactic panels provide the visitor with general background information on each historical period and civilization represented in the galleries. In the guide, on the other hand, the curators have chosen the most important works of art in the Museum's collection, have interpreted their art historical significance, and have evaluated how they reflect the civilization represented in each gallery.

Each section of the guide is identified by a coloured divider with a photograph of a representative object from the gallery. The colour and object correspond to those used on the freestanding orientation elements in the Museum and on the directional signs. With the aid of this colour coding system, and with the map inserted at the end of the guide, the visitor can find the location of each gallery in the Museum.

Fig. 1
Lotbinière, Québec
Two-tiered buffet
late 18th century
pine
gift of Miss Mabel Molson
938.Df.13

Fig. 2
Paul Lambert (called Saint-Paul)
Canadian, 1691-1749
Porringer
early 18th century
silver
Ramsay Traquair Bequest
952.Ds.20

Through the years, the Museum has collected objects and paintings which span Canadian history from the French regime to the present day. In 1929, Dr. F. J. Shepherd created a fund for the purpose of buying Canadian works of art. His example soon was followed by Mr. Robert Lindsay, Miss Harriette J. Macdonnell and Mr. A. Sydney Dawes. At approximately the same time, the Morrice family donated a comprehensive selection of paintings by James Wilson Morrice. The Museum's collection of contemporary Canadian art was expanded through the generosity of Mr. and Mrs. Samuel Bronfman, who granted the Museum an annual fund for the acquisition of works by young Canadian artists aged thirty-five and under.

The influence of European models on early Canadian art and artifacts, and particularly on Québec furniture, is evident throughout the galleries. The late eighteenth-century pine two-tiered buffet (fig. 1) with serpentine pediment, fruit decoration and four doors with shaped panels is of Louis XV derivation. Carved on the two upper doors are baskets of fruits symbolizing abundance . The heart in the center of the baskets suggests that this buffet was offered as a wedding gift. Its elegant mouldings, fische hinges and keyhole escutcheons combine with graceful proportions and balance to make it a very attractive piece of furniture.

Canadian artists of the past also exercised their creativity as silversmiths. An early eighteenth-century silver porringer (fig. 2) came into the Museum as part of the Ramsay Traquair bequest. Two marks identify it as the work of Paul Lambert, called Saint-Paul. The first, consisting of the letters P.L., a flower and a star in a scroll, undoubtedly is that of Lambert; the origin of the second mark is more difficult to determine. The letters S.P. with a crown and a flower in a scroll are thought to be the initials of Samuel Payne (1696-1732), also a silversmith and a contemporary of Lambert. The presence of both marks could indicate that the porringer was the result of a collaboration between Lambert and Payne around 1730. The monogram surrounded with ferns and topped with a crown which appears on the body leads one to believe that the object might have belonged to a noble family.

Fig. 3
Jean-Baptiste Roy-Audy
Canadian, 1778-1848
Portrait of Madame Ranvoyzé
oil on canvas
about 1838
gift of F. Cleveland Morgan
936.1261

At the beginning of the nineteenth century, painters were commissioned by both the Church and the bourgeoisie, hence the large number of portraits and religious subjects produced during this period. Most of the artists were either of European birth or training. *The Portrait of Madame Ranvoyzé* (fig. 3) attributed to Jean-Baptiste Roy-Audy represents Françoise Filion, wife of Etienne Ranvoyzé, brother of the silversmith François Ranvoyzé. Born in Charlesbourg, Québec,

Roy-Audy began his artistic career around 1815. He had received his entire training in Québec; this was rather unusual at the time. In this portrait, Roy-Audy concentrates mainly on the facial features of his model, thus expressing in a forceful manner the sitter's character. The monochrome background sets off the personality of Mme Ranvoyzé.

Fig. 4
Antoine-Sébastien Plamondon
Canadian, 1804-1895
Preparation for the Flagellation
oil on canvas
1837
Horsley and Annie Townsend
    Bequest
961.1323

The Church in Québec soon became the most important sponsor for sculptors, painters, cabinetmakers and silversmiths. The *Preparation for the Flagellation of Christ* (fig. 4) by Antoine-Sébastien Plamondon was part of a series commissioned by Notre-Dame Church of Montréal. Several other Stations of the Cross from this same series are in the Museum's collection. Antoine Plamondon, born near Québec City, received his early training in the studio of the Québec painter, Joseph Légaré. Later, in Paris, he was a pupil of Paulin Guérin, a disciple of David. Under these influences, his style acquired an unmistakably classical touch. The *Flagellation* was inspired by a work of the French painter, Jacques Stella (1596-1657) which Plamondon had come to know through an engraving by Claudine Bouzonnet-Stella. Plamondon has eliminated the spectators in the original composition in order to emphasize the solitude of Christ at the hands of His torturers who are disrobing Him and tying Him to the column. The instruments of flagellation are depicted in the foreground. To the left, the artist has added a pedestal with a piece of cloth and a helmet. The sparseness of the background, the dramatic posture of the figures as well as their anatomical types, derived from ancient sculpture, reflect David's Neo-classicist influence.

Fig. 5
Canada, Gaspé Peninsula
Crucifix
18th century
pine
Horsley and Annie Townsend
   Bequest
965.Df.1

Fig. 6
Cornelius Krieghoff
born in Holland, active in Canada,
  1815-1872
Montmorency Falls
oil on canvas
1853
Charlotte Thomson Bequest
  in memory of her husband
  Peter Alfred Thomson
963.1439

In 1965, the Museum was fortunate to repatriate from the United States a polychrome wood sculpture of *Christ on the Cross* (fig. 5). Executed by an eighteenth-century anonymous artist, the crucifix comes from the Gaspé region. It was carved in American pine and bears some traces of the original paint. The lack of proportion between the head and the body, the stylized anatomical features, the simple and sober shapes as well as the technique of adding parts such as the loincloth, are reminiscent of mediaeval sculpture. It is a symbolic image of Christ.

In addition to portraits of dignitaries and religious subjects, the second half of the nineteenth century produced a style of painting reflecting the Québecois joie de vivre, depicting their customs and events of daily life. Cornelius Krieghoff, a Dutch-born painter, was the main exponent of this new trend. The fifteen Krieghoffs in the Museum's collection illustrate most of his favourite themes. These paintings relate in various ways to the lively landscapes of the seventeenth-century Dutch painters. *Montmorency Falls* (fig. 6) was painted in 1853 after the artist moved from Montréal to Québec City. During that year, Krieghoff was to treat the same subject with slight modifications at least three times. In the Museum's painting, we see a frozen basin below the waterfall, with high cliffs under sunny skies in the background. Scattered groups of people are enjoying winter sports, some sleigh riding, others tobogganing down the slopes; still others are chatting or walking.The fresh and transparent colours of the artist's palette add to the anecdotal flavour of this view of Montmorency Falls an artistic quality which distinguishes Krieghoff from his numerous imitators. Through the years, Krieghoff created a whole gallery of typical Canadians garbed in traditional costumes — heavy, homespun overcoats, colourful woolen belts and tuques — depicted in a variety of occupations and characteristic attitudes. This painting constitutes a valuable document of the life and customs of his time.

Fig. 7
Horatio Walker
Canadian, 1858-1938
The Ice Cutters
oil on canvas
1904
gift of Mrs. F. S. Smithers
  in memory of
    Charles Francis Smithers
941.736

In complete accordance with the social and moral standards established by the clergy and tradition-bound elite, a new style of painting devoted to the glorification of rural life appeared toward the end of the nineteenth century. This movement echoed the artistic concepts of the masters of the French School of Barbizon made famous by the paintings of Jean-François Millet. This is reflected in the Québec farm scenes of Horatio Walker. The son of a Listowel, Ontario lumberman, Walker himself was of rural origin. He had left for Toronto at the age of fifteen, and in 1881 embarked on a voyage to Europe where he familiarized himself with the works of Millet and the School of Barbizon. Upon his return from Europe in 1883, he divided his time between New York and Ile d'Orléans, Québec. Like Homer Watson, Horatio Walker became President of the Canadian Art Club. In his painting *The Ice Cutters* (fig. 7), we see three robust countrymen in the process of cutting from the frozen lake blocks of ice to be stored for later use. In the center of the composition a heavy draught horse hauls a large chunk of freshly cut ice. Without ignoring the details of the setting, he concentrates mainly on the human figures. They are painted in dark colours and stand out against the whiteness of the snow. As in most of Walker's paintings, man and animal are depicted working in close harmony. The light of the late afternoon sun shining directly above the horse creates a strange aura suggesting protection or approval from celestial forces as in the style of holy pictures. The transparent blue colour of the ice, together with the reflection of the sunshine on the snow, produce a luminous effect. Other landscape painters, such as Suzor-Côté, Maurice Cullen and Clarence Gagnon, later carried on this style in a more Impressionistic fashion.

At the turn of the century, in the quiet of his mountain retreat at Saint-Hilaire, Ozias Leduc created a richly individual oeuvre

Fig. 8
Ozias Leduc
Canadian, 1864-1955
L'heure mauve
oil on paper mounted on canvas
1921
gift of Mrs. Samuel Bronfman,
    O.B.E., in honour of the 70th
    birthday of her husband,
    Samuel Bronfman
961.1320

almost unique in the history of Canadian painting. Although his fame in the province was based mainly on his paintings for churches, Leduc also created small easel compositions, still lifes, landscapes and portraits. After a trip to Paris in 1897, Leduc's work showed traces of Impressionism and Art Nouveau; in 1912 his style took a decisive turn toward Symbolism. Leduc was the interpreter of silent things, of clouded skies, images of suspended time, of dreams of the infinite. In his poetic texts as well as in many of his pictures, Ozias Leduc evoked the mysteries of afterlife and expressed his obsession with the fatal passing of time. This is the theme of *L'heure mauve* (fig. 8), painted in 1921, in which Leduc depicts the end of the day and its subdued light. There is a mellow and almost religious silence in these few square feet of dull snow, fallen branches and dead leaves. By eliminating the horizon, the artist imbues with mystery this small portion of land situated in an imaginary framework. This picture suggests a photographic close-up; the sinuous curves of the branches also reflect the influence of Art Nouveau. The brush lingers on the undulations of the snow and carefully depicts the crumpled leaves and their subtle muted tones.

Fig. 9
James Wilson Morrice
Canadian, 1865-1924
The Racecourse, Vincennes
oil on canvas
1906
J. W. Tempest Fund
932.635

A comprehensive selection of the paintings of James Wilson Morrice allows the viewer to pursue an in-depth study of his development. Morrice, who had established himself in Paris in 1890, became the first Canadian artist to gain international recognition. While studying at the Académie Julian, Morrice became acquainted with American artists such as Robert Henri, Maurice Prendergast, William Glackens and Whistler, who exercised a marked influence on his art. His European paintings show Impressionist, Symbolist and Fauve trends, while his Canadian oeuvre establishes him as a forerunner of the Group of Seven. While in Canada he often worked with Cullen and Brymner. An afternoon at the races inspired his *Racecourse, Vincennes* (fig. 9) in the European series. The figure to the right is thought to be the artist himself, while the woman with her dog in the center, turning toward the painter, would be Léa Cadoret, the artist's favourite model. This picture shows some of the characteristics that contributed to the fame of the Impressionists, in particular, the freedom of the brushwork and the light touch. The subject matter itself recalls some of Degas' best known works. This painting is believed to have been executed in 1906 after one of the trips to Venice which Morrice had made in the company of his fellow countryman, Maurice Cullen. In Venice, he discovered the subtle light of the Italian environment. After 1905, Morrice progressively moved away from the somber tone which characterized his first paintings. Little by little he replaced the heavy brushwork of his earlier works with thin layers of colour. These layers in certain areas allow the white canvas to show through, as may be observed in the sky of our landscape (fig. 9). The artist's palette contains warmer and clearer tones. In contrast to the Impressionists, Morrice painted his pictures in his studio, as visual expressions of recollections; their execution does not follow immediate perception. Morrice is in fact a sensitive poet more akin to the Symbolists.

Fig. 10
James Wilson Morrice
Canadian, 1865-1924
The Old Holton House, Montréal
oil on canvas
about 1909
puchase, John W. Tempest Fund
915.129

Every winter until the death of his parents in 1914, Morrice spent a few months in Canada. He illustrated the dull grey winter skies, the Québec streets with sleighs and isolated walkers, and the frozen Saint Lawrence. The *Old Holton House, Montreal* (fig. 10), was painted by Morrice after a pencil sketch also in the Museum's collection. This house, which was demolished in 1911, stood on the corner of Sherbrooke Street and Ontario Avenue, the site of the Museum today. This painting was the first of Morrice's works to be acquired by the Museum (1915). It is interesting to note the similarity between this composition and his *Racecourse, Vincennes*. One finds the same long fence across the entire width of the picture; in front of it, in approximately the same place, stand the people. In addition, the old house is the focal point of the scene, just as the Vincennes cluster of trees is the center of that painting. This work marks a new stage in Morrice's development; he now covers the entire surface with a transparent layer of paint. The drawing is freer, colours fresher and the brushwork more flowing. These qualities were to be developed further during his numerous trips in the sunny regions of the Atlantic and Mediterranean such as Cuba, Jamaica, Martinique, Morocco and, finally, Tunisia where he died in 1924.

Fig. 11
Arthur Lismer
Canadian, England 1885-
 Montréal 1969
Cathedral Mountain
oil on canvas
1928
gift of A. Sidney Dawes
959.1219

In the spring of 1920, the Art Gallery of Toronto presented an exhibition which ensured official recognition of the Group of Seven whose fame would henceforth spread across Canada. This was the first essentially Canadian school of painting. For the first time, the works of Arthur Lismer, J. E. H. MacDonald, Frederick Varley, Lawren S. Harris, A. Y. Jackson, Frank H. Johnston and Franklin Carmichael were assembled in a comprehensive manner. There was nothing arbitrary in the grouping of these artists. For many years, they had been working together with Tom Thomson, who died in 1917. Arthur Lismer, one of the pioneers of the Group, had come to Canada from Sheffield, England, and settled in Toronto in 1911. He soon became friends with Tom Thomson and Lawren Harris, whom he met at the Arts and Letters Club in Toronto. In 1941, he became Dean of the School of Art and Design of the Montreal Museum of Fine Arts, a post he occupied until his death in 1969. Among the numerous drawings and paintings by Lismer in the Museum collection, *Cathedral Mountain* (fig. 11) best illustrates the poetic goal of the Group: the expression of the awe-inspiring beauty of our magnificent landscapes through a new and typically Canadian vocabulary. This painting was executed in his studio from a sketch drawn near Lakes Moraine and O'Hara during a trip to the Rockies.

Lismer has painted the mountain from a distance in order to depict its full splendour. It appears as a giant heap of many stone blocks resting solidly upon one another. The towering majesty of the mountain recalls that of a Gothic cathedral. A stormy sky with menacing clouds caps the summit of the mountain, emphasizing the powerful character of the Rockies. Lismer has stylized the mountain structure and retains only its volume. He expresses with great feeling and depth his emotion at this imposing view. Somber tones of brown and grey are in perfect harmony with the general atmosphere of the composition. Lismer's goal, like that of his companions, was to bring the viewers of his works to share nature's poetry and spiritual beauty.

At a time when the nationalistic ideal was a major influence in the artistic circles of Toronto, Bertram Brooker became one of the first Canadian painters to introduce abstraction in his work. In a discussion of a series of his formal compositions exhibited at the Arts and Letters Club in 1927, he stated as his purpose the visual reproduction of musical sensations without any recourse to figurative elements. In this series, Brooker adopted Kandinsky's concepts on the meaning of art and its strong intellectual implications. The painting *Kneeling Figure* (fig. 12), dated between 1937 and 1940, cannot be compared to abstract works of the twenties; rather, it is a vision of the human body influenced by the first Cubist works of Braque and Picasso. One of Brooker's early encounters with Cubism occurred in 1927 when the Art Gallery of Ontario held an exhibition of works by Duchamp, Mondrian and Stella. A nude woman, kneeling in the manner of a starting runner, occupies most of the composition. Two long diagonal lines cut the figure; one from top to bottom, the other, almost halfway across the picture. Although at certain points these lines indicate the position of the

Fig. 12
Bertram Brooker
Canadian, 1888-1955
Kneeling Figure
oil on canvas
1940
Horsley and Annie Townsend
  Bequest
1973.17

limbs, their main purpose is to create an arbitrary division of the body into several sections. In this fashion, Brooker creates an ambiguous spatial structure which places the anatomical features of the body and the background on the same level. The juxtaposed brushstrokes do not reproduce the tactile quality of the woman's skin but instead give it the same value as the background. Brooker does not resort to the traditional monochrome tones of the Cubists but it is evident that the degrees of light are more important to him than the rendering of real colours.

The return of Alfred Pellan to Québec in the spring of 1940 marked a decisive turn in the development of contemporary Canadian art. The fourteen years he spent working with the great masters of the School of Paris provided the painter with an in-depth artistic knowledge. He was regarded by many as a liberator from the academism still prevalent in Québec painting at that time. Retracing the steps of his evolution is difficult because of the abundance and diversity of his works. The portraits and still lifes of his early days were followed by surrealistic and poetic compositions exploding with rich and lively colours, fantasy and joie de vivre. *Jardin volcanique* (fig. 13),

Fig. 13
Alfred Pellan
Canadian, 1906-
Jardin volcanique
oil, sand and tobacco on canvas
1960
gift of the Volunteer Committee
960.1242

painted in 1960, deserves a special mention in the production of this period. It relates to a series of six paintings done two years earlier on the theme of the garden and the primary colours: the *Blue Garden,* the *Yellow Garden,* the *Red Garden,* the *Green Garden,* the *Orange Garden* and the *Purple Garden.* These large compositions develop one of the major elements of Pellan's subject matter: nature. Pellan has never adopted pure abstraction, preferring to experiment with various techniques or means of expression which have led him to a transformation of figurative art. *Jardin volcanique* is probably the result of such an experiment. The artist here eliminates all reference to traditional landscapes. He concentrates on a portion of the ground which spreads into the flattened space of the picture with little or no perspective, as in a child's drawing. Unusual materials such as powdered silica, bits of dried tobacco and Polyfilla mixed into a rough paste, are combined to form the relief of the volcanic soil. From this scraped and kneaded material he creates delicately contoured flowers. These carefully structured shapes are alive with vibrant colours. As expected in this garden of fire, a vivid red is the dominant colour. The design of the flowers is delineated with blue, yellow, purple and green hues, suggesting electrical vibrations.

In August 1948, Paul-Emile Borduas published his manifesto *Refus Global,* a protest against the ideals of the elite who, in his opinion, were to blame for the artistic as well as intellectual stagnation of the Québecois. This defiance was reflected in his art with the greatest freedom of imagination and technique within a surrealistic inspiration based on the writings of André Breton. Borduas initiated the Automatist movement which was to exert such a marked influence on the development of Québec painting. According to the

Fig. 14
Paul-Émile Borduas
Canadian, 1905-1960
Les carquois fleuris
oil on canvas
1947
gift of Mr. and Mrs. Maurice
   Chartré
962.1343

definition of a Parisian critic, Leon Degand, "Automatism is a beneficial submission to the dictates of spontaneity, a pictorial lack of discipline, technical chance, romanticism of the brush and lyrical superabundance". *Les carquois fleuris* (fig. 14), painted in 1947, is part of a series which marks an important stage in the artist's development. The expression "Automatism" was employed for the first time in 1947 as the title of an exhibition held in the Palais du Luxembourg in Paris. Combining various pictorial techniques, Borduas composes a picture showing alternatively the unconscious forces of expression and a desire to enclose the poetical message within a formal structure. The creation of the work could be divided into two intertwined moments. The background applied with the brush covers the entire surface of the canvas. Tones of brown, green, blue and grey in horizontal layers mingle and produce an indefinite space bathed in gloomy light. The expression of subconscious impulses is shown in the foreground. With brush and spatula the artist vaguely suggests Indian quivers filled with arrows. The hand of the painter moves with great freedom. The lightly grouped objects placed at different levels seem to be floating in space without any real depth, thus emphasizing the distance from the background. In future experiments with subconsciously-controlled painting, Borduas gradually eliminated both the distance between the two planes and the recognizable objects. His oeuvre, one of the most articulate in Québec painting, laid the groundwork for all future abstract art in this province. In 1950, Borduas saw in Montréal an exhibition of abstract works by de Kooning, Gorky, Motherwell, Rothko and Jackson Pollock. After his one-man exhibition in New York in 1953, Borduas drew closer to American masters of Abstract Expressionism such as Pollock.

Fig. 15
Alex Colville
Canadian, 1920-
Church and Horse
acrylic on masonite
1964
Horsley and Annie Townsend
  Bequest
966.1529

While avant-garde artists of the forties were introducing abstract art to Québec, Ontario and a few western areas, New Brunswick artist David Alexander Colville centered his experiments around the observation of nature. These efforts led to a striking form of painting which eventually was called "magic realism". A feeling of surpassing reality emanates from Colville's paintings. *Church and Horse* (fig. 15), painted in 1964, brings together the essential characteristics of Alex Colville's style. An austere little Protestant church without windows is in the center of the canvas. The door is closed and indicates no sign of life. In the foreground a brown horse is galloping toward the open gate of the church fence. To the far right is a lone stone monument. Each of these elements is projected against a grey sky and a narrow strip of grassy terrain. An almost entirely overcast sky sheds a grey aura over the scene. There is a sharp contrast here between the vitality of the animal and the imposing static quality of the church. The horse seems anxious to escape from some impending danger. The relationship between the various elements of the scene seems carefully measured. This geometric display reinforces the impression of immobility and confers on the whole the austerity of a symbolic presentation. While paying scrupulous attention to the minor details of his brushwork, Colville retains only those details which he deems significant.

The continued interest of the Museum in Canadian artistic production has resulted in the last decade in the significant growth of the contemporary art collection. Its variety is evident in other galleries of the Museum. Abstract paintings, sculptures and graphics bear witness to the activity of the Toronto *Painters Eleven* at the end of the fifties, as well as the Montréal *Plasticiens* during the sixties. Examples of the *Op* and *Pop* movements and even minimal and conceptual art also have been added to the collection.

Inuit and Amerindian Art

The Museum's collection of Indian and Inuit art was begun in 1917, when a number of American Indian objects and one artifact of Northwest Coast origin were acquired. Since that time the collection has grown to include artifacts and art objects from tribes spanning the entire North American continent. In recent years the Museum has concentrated on the acquisition of objects representing both the cultural heritage and modern production of Canadian native peoples. Northwest Coast Indian and Inuit art are particularly well represented in the collection.

Inuit and Amerindian art is the product of many different peoples whose cultures varied from those of simple hunting groups to complex agricultural societies which were and still are conditioned by different religious, social, economic and geographic factors. The ancestors of the Eskimo and Indian groups of North America migrated from Asia some 25,000 years ago by way of the Bering land bridge that once joined Siberia and Alaska. Human occupation in the far northern regions can be divided into three periods: Pre-Dorset, beginning around 2500 BC and fading toward 800 BC; Dorset, stretching from 800 BC to 1300 AD; and the Thule culture, which lasted until the coming of the European whalers at the beginning of the eighteenth century. Traditional Eskimo carving was practised within a

shamanistic discipline as a means of appeasing the spirits of the animals whose flesh was so necessary for survival. With the disappearance of whaling and the commercialization of the hunt, carvings ceased to serve a ritualistic function and became primarily decorative, casual objects of a secular nature. An ornately carved nineteenth-century cribbage board in the Museum's collection illustrates the synthesis of Eskimo craftsmanship with the culture of the white man, or *kablunait.*

The contemporary phase of carving among the Inuit — the name used by the Eskimos to refer to themselves and meaning "The People" — had its beginnings in the winter of 1948-49, when the Canadian artist James Houston, on a visit to a settlement at Port Harrison, astutely recognized the artistic talent of the inhabitants and set about finding a market for their work in the south. The subsequent renaissance of Eskimo carving has succeeded in providing not only a new source of income for the Inuit, but also has fostered a renewed spiritual and cultural self-esteem.

Today the artist in the Arctic gives to his people and to the white man a vital record of old hunting ways, a visual rendering of the spirit world which was thought to govern Eskimo life, and a representation of customs, fables and adventures from the recent past. One such event, a desperate voyage undertaken by a group of forty Eskimos, is the subject of *The Migration* (fig. 16) by Joe Talirunili of Povungnituk. This sculpture, depicting a boat and passengers, was carved of grey stone in 1964. As a young boy, Joe Talirunili was

Fig. 16
Joe Talirunili
Canadian, 1899-
The Migration
grey stone, bone and skin
1964
gift of John G. McConnell
1974.Aa.2

part of an Eskimo band which had become trapped on a drifting ice floe; to escape death by starvation and exposure, they were forced to set sail for a distant island in a hastily-fashioned *umiak*, a family or woman's boat made of animal skins. At seventy-eight, Joe Talirunili is the sole living survivor today; the names of many of the other participants are inscribed on the hull of the boat. The massive quality of the sculpture conveys a sense of the difficulty with which the heavily-laden boat stayed a-float. The extreme crowding of the figures, together with their postures and facial expressions, speak eloquently and dramatically of the anxiety and desperation of the voyagers. The figure of a young boy, presumably the artist, can be detached from the group. A print-maker as well as a sculptor, Talirunili has recorded the same incident in a stone cut entitled *Return of the Survivors from the Floating Ice*. These individualistic works serve as a monument to the courage and tenacity of the Inuit people.

Fig. 17
Parr
Canadian, 1889-1969
Harpooning Walrus
etching
1963
Gr.1975.16

Unlike carving, which is an indigenous art form practised by the Inuit from earliest times, the origins of printmaking in the Arctic are recent. Again, credit must be given to James Houston, who introduced the technique of the stone cut to the Inuit of Cape Dorset in 1957. The following year, these same artists began working with stenciled prints and finally, in 1961, they experimented with engraving directly into copper plates. Each type of printmaking calls for the reapplication of an already existing Eskimo skill: the stone cut has affinities with carving, the stencil cut is related to the adornment of clothing by the art of skin appliqué, and engraving has its roots in the tradition of incised decoration on bone and horn.

Parr, an Eskimo from Cape Dorset, was one of the first northern artists to experiment with the technique of engraving. In 1963, he produced a number of etchings utilizing the distinctive technique of hatching demonstrated in *Harpooning Walrus* (fig. 17). As in almost all his art, the subject matter is drawn from his experience as a hunter and kayakman. Parr himself executed the incisions for all his etchings directly on the plates without prior sketches. His stone cuts, however, follow the Eskimo practice of dividing the work of the artist, blockcutter and printer into separate functions. Two hunters, accompanied by their dogs, have just speared a walrus. Though simple and direct, the work transmits to its viewer an extraordinary vitality which permits him to share in the movement and excitement of the hunt. The hunter has thrown up his arms in joy at his success. His partner, arms extended, has already begun to move toward the disabled animal. The dogs bark in unison. Through art that is disarming and pure in its directness, Parr has isolated a moment in the life of the Eskimo and rendered it universally comprehensible.

Indian art styles show a great diversity throughout the North American continent. Skills such as pottery-making, wood, bone and shell carving, bead- and feather-work, basketry and the graphic arts constitute a rich artistic heritage that has survived for more than a millennium. The development of more or less homogeneous art styles and tech-

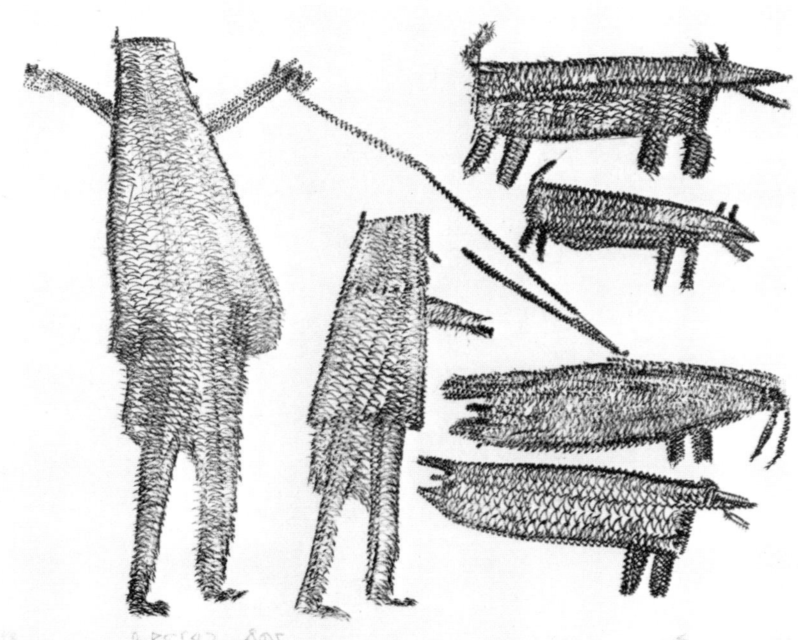

Fig. 18
Canada
Athabaskan or Cree Indian
bow loom
porcupine quills, wood, cotton,
  thread and leather
purchase, Horsley and Annie
  Townsend Bequest
1975.Ab.1

niques are the result of the isolation experienced by many of the Indian groups throughout their history. In Canada, Indian tribes generally are divided into three broad groups coinciding with established linguistic, physiographic and climatic regions: the Eastern Woodlands tribes, the Plains Indians and the Northwest Coast cultures.

The Eastern Woodlands territory covers a vast quadrilateral-shaped area stretching from Edmonton in the west to Newfoundland in the east, and from Fort Chimo in the north to Lake Erie in the south. Although crops were cultivated to some extent, the majority of Eastern Woodlands Indians were hunters and fishermen belonging to the Algonkian linguistic group. Dialects of this language were spoken by the Micmac, Malecite, Montagnais, Meskapi, Algonquin, Ojibway, Cree and perhaps Beothuk tribes. In the Great Lakes region dwelt people of the Iroquois linguistic group, consisting of the Huron, Petun, Neutrals and the Five Nations Iroquois (Mohawk, Oneida, Onondaga, Cayuga and Seneca), all of whom participated in a thriving agrarian way of life. In the Museum's collection, the Indians of the Eastern Woodlands are represented by such artifacts as a nineteenth-century "smiling grandfather" mask, probably from the Seneca tribe, a ceremonial gun stock, and a number of Algonquin baskets.

The Canadian Prairies extend from near Winnipeg in Manitoba to the foothills of the Rocky Mountains. For more than 10,000 years, the life and culture of the inhabitants of this area depended upon the bison. Tribes of Blackfoot, Peigan, Gros Ventre, Assiniboin and a branch of the Cree pursued the herds in a perpetual quest for food. Dogs were their only beasts of burden until approximately 1700, when horses were acquired by trading with southern bands. The newly acquired wealth

and leisure following the change from a static to a mobile culture, together with the introduction of European trade goods, fostered the development of creative arts usually associated with religion, war or personal ostentation. A rough, bow-shaped loom made from a stripped, bent tree branch (fig. 18) was used in the production of porcupine quill decorative work. The finest quills were taken from the underside of the animal, dyed, flattened and woven into attractively patterned strips to be sewn onto articles of clothing. Dyes were extracted from natural products such as vegetables, moss, soil and charcoal. The quills were locked into a simple checker weave. Of necessity, the patterns were composed of angular forms such as diamonds and crosses, as in the Museum's example. However, the rhythmical repetition and harmony of the soft colours combine to temper the geometrical severity of the design.

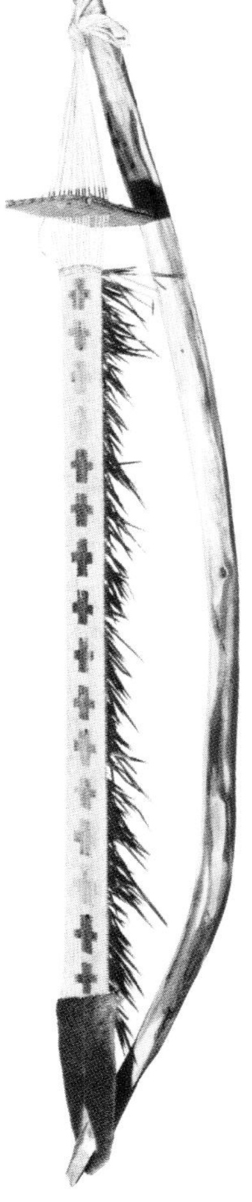

Fig. 19
Canada, Queen Charlotte Islands,
   B.C.
Chilkat tribe
blanket
mountain goat's wool
gift of The Canadian Handicrafts
   Guild
919.Ab.2

The Northwest Coast area consists of a narrow 1,500-mile landstrip of temperate evergreen forests, Pacific Ocean off-coast islands and fjord-like inlets stretching from the Gulf of Alaska to the southern tip of Vancouver Island. This region was inhabited by the sedentary fishing groups of Tlingit, Tsimshian, Haida, Kwakiutl, Nootka, Salish and Chinook Indians, whose art fulfilled both social and religious purposes. On the social plane, the artistic motivation of the Pacific Coast Indians included the desire for prestige, vanity, pride in craftsmanship, and the giving of gifts. Through the display of heraldic crests of kinship groups and the proclaiming of special privileges, their art served as a representation of social organization. Haida totem poles were the most prominent expressions of this need to assert high social standing but other possessions, ranging from canoes to spoons, also were adorned with crest patterns. Since the main purpose of the crest was easy identification, the northern artist acquired a conventionalized system of indicating crest animals through the selection of distinctive features. Although highly stylized, the totemic motifs depicted on the Museum's fine Chilkat blanket (fig. 19) indicate that it once belonged to a member of the Grizzly Bear clan. The blanket was woven in the nineteenth century by the women of the Chilkat tribe, a division of the Tlingit group, from a painted pattern prepared by a man. Mountain goat's wool, beaten and wound around a core of cedar bark twine, was dyed pale blue, yellow and dark brown. An unsophisticated shuttleless loom was used to execute the design. The ground of the blanket is divided into three parts; the middle section contains the

vocabulary of geometric design elements representing the animal figure. A human-like face stands out in bold relief. The side panels contain similar geometric patterns arranged with a regard for symmetry, attesting to its origins in the representational painting of the Northern Pacific Coast tribes. On the death of a chief or important owner, the blanket was placed on the grave and allowed to disintegrate as a mark of esteem.

Through forceful and original religious art, an attempt was made to give tangible form to the supernatural beings of the universe, thereby allowing for the ritual dramatization of man's relation with them. A number of dance cycles were performed, calling for a wide array of different masks, headdresses and costumes. A small, well-modelled wooden mask (fig. 20) possibly from the Kwakiutl tribe of the central Northwest Coast region, could have been worn either on its own or affixed to the front of a ceremonial headdress. Black paint emphasizes the heavy brows, and traces of red remain on the lips and nose. Although lacking the characteristic recurved nose, the

band of haliotis shells encircling the face suggests that it is a representation of the sun. Light reflecting from these plaques simulates the rays of the sun. The deep blue-green lustre of the shells indicates that they were procured through trade either from California or Japan.

The native art of North America springs from rich and complex sources. A long history of adaptation to changing climate, geography and economic base, as well as a continuing process of cultural synthesis and exposure to technology, lie behind almost every object exhibited.

**Ancient
Near East**

Fig. 21
Egypt, Pre-Dynastic Period
4000-3200 BC
Vase
clay
gift of Miss Mabel Molson
925.B.1.

Archaeologists have discovered art and artifacts in Egypt which are dated as early as the fourth millennium before Christ, but the Dynastic era, the period of the recorded history of Egypt, begins in ca. 3200 BC. At this time, the first kings of Egypt united the settlements of northern (Lower) and southern (Upper) Egypt into a unified kingdom. Egyptian history is divided into four periods: the Archaic (3200-2680 BC), Old (2680-2565 BC), Middle (2040-1786 BC) and New (1570-1085 BC) Kingdoms. Between the last three epochs, two intermediate periods, each lasting approximately two centuries, mark the fall of Egypt from a strong, unified state into internal turmoil, when the country was reduced to a number of smaller kingdoms ruled by local princes. In the latter stages of Egypt's long history the country was infiltrated by foreign populations. After a period during the 26th Dynasty known as the "Saite Renaissance", when indigenous culture flourished again for a brief time, Egypt was invaded and dominated twice by the Persians (525 and 341 BC), the Macedonians under Alexander the Great (332 BC), and later by the Romans under Octavian (30 BC), when Egypt became essentially a province of the Roman Empire.

The Museum's collection of Egyptian art began in 1917 with a gift from F. Cleveland Morgan of three Coptic textile fragments. Today, the collection includes approximately one hundred art objects, spanning all periods of Egypt's artistic achievement.

A small, two-handled pottery vase (fig. 21) dating to the Pre-Dynastic era (4000-3200 BC) with delicately painted flamingoes and zig-zag bands constitutes a fine example of how Egyptian art, from its earliest beginnings, re-interpreted images drawn from a close observation of nature into a pleasing decorative scheme. This tendency again can be seen clearly in several of the Museum's relief fragments from the Middle Kingdom temples at Lisht and Deir el-Bahari which depict gracefully sculpted flora and fauna. This acute awareness of the natural world and its transformation into a highly decorative art is — together with the close association of the arts and funerary cults — a primary factor in the development of the Egyptian style.

From the "Saite Renaissance", that brief period of national unity following an Assyrian sack of the major Egyptian centers of Memphis and Thebes in the mid-seventh century BC, comes a bronze statuette of Sekhmet. Sekhmet was the much-feared goddess who in Egyptian mythology attacked and nearly exterminated the human race. The detailed modelling of the figure shows her with a lion's head and unusually robust anatomy, evoking in this way her aggressive disposition.

Fig. 22
Egypt, Persian Period,
  Dynasty XXX
Offering to Osiris from
Nektanebo II
Temple of Isis
Behbeit el-Higara
Horsley and Annie Townsend and
  Gilman Cheney Bequest
964.B.1

The sunken relief fragment (fig. 22) representing King Nektanebo II making an offering to Osiris (the god of death and resurrection) was executed during the 30th Dynasty, a period of great political upheaval between the two Persian invasions of Egypt. Nektanebo II was the last native-born Egyptian to rule Egypt and during his reign several important building projects were undertaken. This fragment was found at Behbeit el-Higara, a town in the Delta region, the birthplace of the King, where he built a temple dedicated to the goddess Isis. Nektanebo is represented in the center of the fragment, with hands raised in the act of offering a gift to Osiris, to the right. The second figure of Osiris to the left belongs to another scene. The rhythmical arrangement of the figures and their frozen poses convey the sacredness of this solemn meeting of Nektanebo and Osiris in the next world. Although the relief was never completed (we can see that Nektanebo's offering and Osiris' sceptre are missing), its execution is of a very high quality. The subtle modelling of the images is accentuated by the shadows cast by the delicate outlines of each figure. Like the artists of the "Saite Renaissance", this artist has emulated the traditionally high level of craftsmanship of the earlier and more stable epochs of Egypt's history.

Fig. 23
Egypt, Coptic Period
Capital from a convent,
Cheikh Abâda
limestone
about 5th century AD
Horsley and Annie Townsend
   Bequest
959.B.2

Coptic art, the final phase of Egyptian art, combines Hellenistic (or Roman), Eastern and Early Christian influences with traditional Egyptian forms and subjects. Among the Museum's significant collection of Coptic textiles (an important medium in this period), a representation of a hawk-like bird shows the influence of Hellenistic art in the careful attention paid to naturalistic details such as the colouring around the eyes, the texture of the feathers and the shading of the beak. Hellenistic and Roman portraits influenced the production of late Egyptian "mummy portraits". These portraits, painted on wood with a wax mixture known as "encaustic", were highly individualized, realistic portrayals painted during the lifetime of the deceased. At his death, they were fitted into a "window" cut into his mummy case. A series of three relief fragments decorated with an animal frieze (fig. 23) originating from a fourth-century AD Coptic convent in central Egypt derive their style from Middle Eastern prototypes and are characterized by symmetry and repetition of motifs. The decorative elements along the lower portions of the reliefs, as well as the leaf patterns in the animal frieze, derive ultimately from Roman models, and these motifs eventually became part of the tradition of early Christian art.

Mesopotamian art emerged and developed at almost the same time as Egyptian art, but was not influenced by it until the Assyrian invasion of Egypt in the middle of the seventh century BC. Mesopotamia, located in the valley between the Tigres and Euphrates Rivers in the so-called "Fertile Crescent", was geographically unprotected and throughout its history was infiltrated by many neighbouring populations such as the Hittites, Aramaeans and Phoenicians. This complex of ethnic elements means a great artistic diversity quite different from the homogeneous development of Egyptian art. Geographically, ancient Mesopotamia is divided roughly into two areas: Sumeria and Babylonia to the south and Assyria to the north. The Sumerians dominated the area between ca. 3100-1950 BC and the Babylonians between ca. 1950 and 1100 BC. The Assyrians began to gain political power from ca. 2000 BC and controlled Mesopotamia from 900 BC until the Persian conquest of the area in 612 BC. Because of this almost continuous political upheaval, only a few figures, such as the Babylonian King Hammurabi (ca. 1793-1750 BC), have been remembered as major historical figures.

Fig. 24
Assyria
Eagle-headed Winged Genie
  Fertilizing the Sacred Tree.
  Northwest Palace of
  Ashurnasirpal II, Nimrud
gypseous alabaster
about 877 BC
Miss Olive Hosmer and Horsley
  and Annie Townsend Bequest
964.Ea.3

The artistic diversity of Mesopotamian art makes a characterization of its style difficult but, generally speaking, its compositions and figures are static and rigid. Like the Egyptians, Mesopotamian artists drew many details of their art by closely observing the world around them, but Mesopotamian art has none of the delicate, sometimes lyrical, elegance of Egyptian art. Instead, it impresses the viewer with its awe-inspiring, almost menacing quality. These elements most certainly characterize an Assyrian relief fragment (fig. 24) dating to ca. 877 BC, the height of Assyrian power in the Near East. The sculpture, of gypseous alabaster, was part of the wall decoration of an audience room in the Northwest Palace of King Ashurnasirpal II at Nimrud, one of the most important building projects of late Assyrian civilization. The eagle-headed winged genie on our fragment is a typical creation of Mesopotamian art; half-man, half-animal figures guard doorways and lintels throughout this and other palaces. He holds a pail and an ear of corn, and is in the act of blessing or fertilizing the highly stylized "Sacred Tree". Across the upper part of the relief, cuneiform characters describe the achievements of the King and the Assyrian Empire. Along the left edge of the panel, roughly sawed off by nineteenth-century excavators, we can see the end of a toe at the bottom of the panel and a tip of an ear of corn near the top. This means that originally the tree was flanked symmetrically by two genii. The piece matching this one is now at the Wadsworth Atheneum in Hartford, Connecticut.

The subject of this relief is related to the myth of Tammuz, the Assyrian god of corn. Like the Egyptian god Osiris, he was cruelly killed and later resurrected to life. The depiction of these scenes at Ashurnasirpal's palace were probably intended to protect the king from evil and death. The figures (which in the palace would have been repeated numerous times along the walls) are arranged in strict symmetry. This composition echoes that of the Egyptian relief of Nektanebo II and, like it, is meant to evoke the solemn relationship of king and deity. Although the sculpture is executed in very shallow relief, the body of the genie has great depth and volume because the muscles of the arms and legs have been boldly delineated and the surfaces subtly rounded.

The decline of Near Eastern art coincides in time with the rise of Greek civilization in the Aegean peninsula. Later, Greco-Roman civilization dominated the development of Western art.

Greek,
Etruscan and
Roman Art

Greek, Etruscan and Roman Art

Fig. 25
attributed to the Nikoxenos Painter
Greek
Dionysus and Two Satyrs
Black Figure Vase
Archaic: about 500 BC
gift of Harry A. Norton
939.Cb.1

The Greeks and Romans bequeathed to mankind a classical heritage which is the basis of our Western civilization. The Aegean Peninsula had been populated since 3000 BC. There were two major high-points of civilization: one between 2200 and 1000 BC when the Mycenaean and Minoan cultures flourished, the second between 800 and 300 BC when Greece was divided into separate city-states, the most important of which were Athens, Corinth and Sparta.

The Museum's collection of Greek and Roman art began in 1918 with the purchase of a Greek vase. Over the years, the collection was enlarged through the donation of the Harry Norton collection of Roman glass in 1952 and, most recently, in 1974 with the purchase of a Roman mosaic of the third century AD.

The Museum owns a considerable number of Greek vases. The art of pottery was developed by the Mycenaeans around 1000 BC. At first, geometric patterns were used. From about the eighth to the end of the sixth century BC, human figures were painted with iron-based liquid clay which was glazed in the kiln and turned black. The finest example of this type, known as the *black figure* style, is a water jug or hydria (fig. 25) attributed to the Nikoxenos painter. He was a member of a workshop in Corinth. Discovered in Vulci, Italy, the vase testifies to the extensive trade the Greeks conducted throughout the Mediterranean. It can be dated around 500 BC, just before the *black figure* technique went out of use.

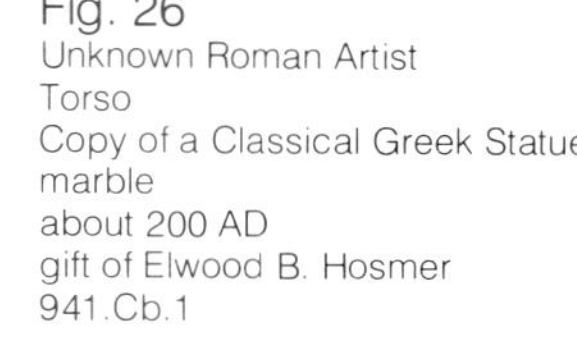

Fig. 26
Unknown Roman Artist
Torso
Copy of a Classical Greek Statue
marble
about 200 AD
gift of Elwood B. Hosmer
941.Cb.1

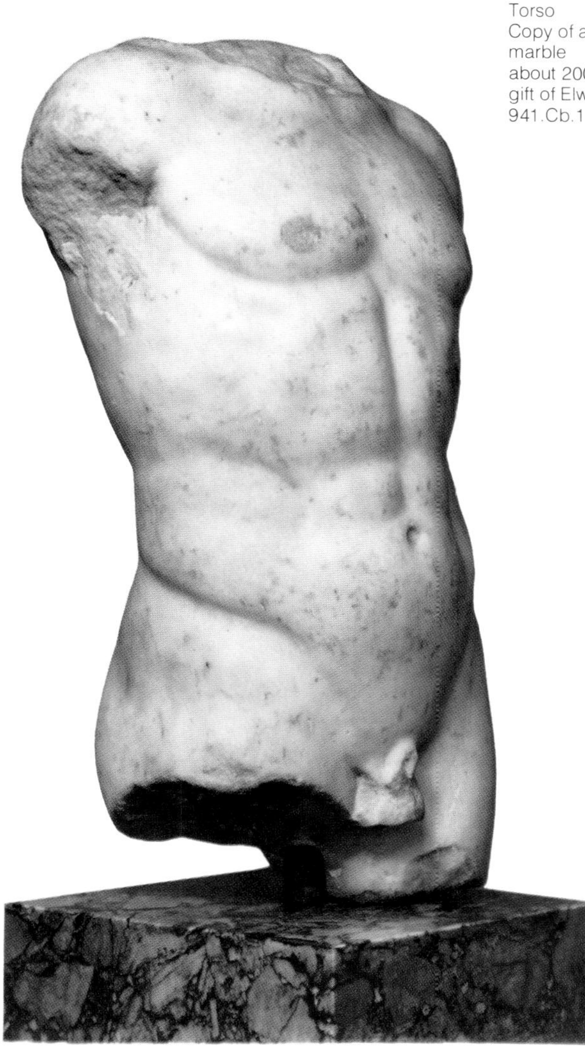

The Greek god of wine, Dionysus, is depicted between two satyrs who are playing the cithara or lute. Like the sculptor of the archaic period, the painter here infused naturalistic anatomical details into a schematic formula for the human figure. All three figures are elongated. Greek painters had discovered techniques to indicate space relationships. Thus, in this vase, the shins and forearms of the two satyrs have been foreshortened. Despite the fact that the heads of the figures are shown in profile, silhouetted in black against the red surface of the clay, the bodies are represented in three-quarter views. One satyr turns to the left, the other to the right. Dionysus himself turns his body to his left. In this way, the artist suggests three-dimensionality.

During the classical period in Greece from the beginning of the fifth through the end of the fourth century BC, the Greek artist achieved a more naturalistic representation of the human body through his study of anatomy. Evidence of this new depiction of the human body in motion is found in a torso in the Museum collection (fig. 26) which is a Roman copy of a Greek work of the fifth century BC. In this torso, the sculptor has depicted the rib cage and muscles in a naturalistic way. He represents the body in contrapposto, an Italian term which describes the position of the human body with the weight resting on one leg, and the other leg free. This position produces animation of the human body structure which evokes a sense of life in the figure. It was used for the first time in the famous *Spear Bearer* by Polycleitos of about 450 BC.

Fig. 27
Unknown Roman Sculptor
Portrait of a Man
marble
copy of Republican work, 100 AD
Special Replacement Fund.
1974.55

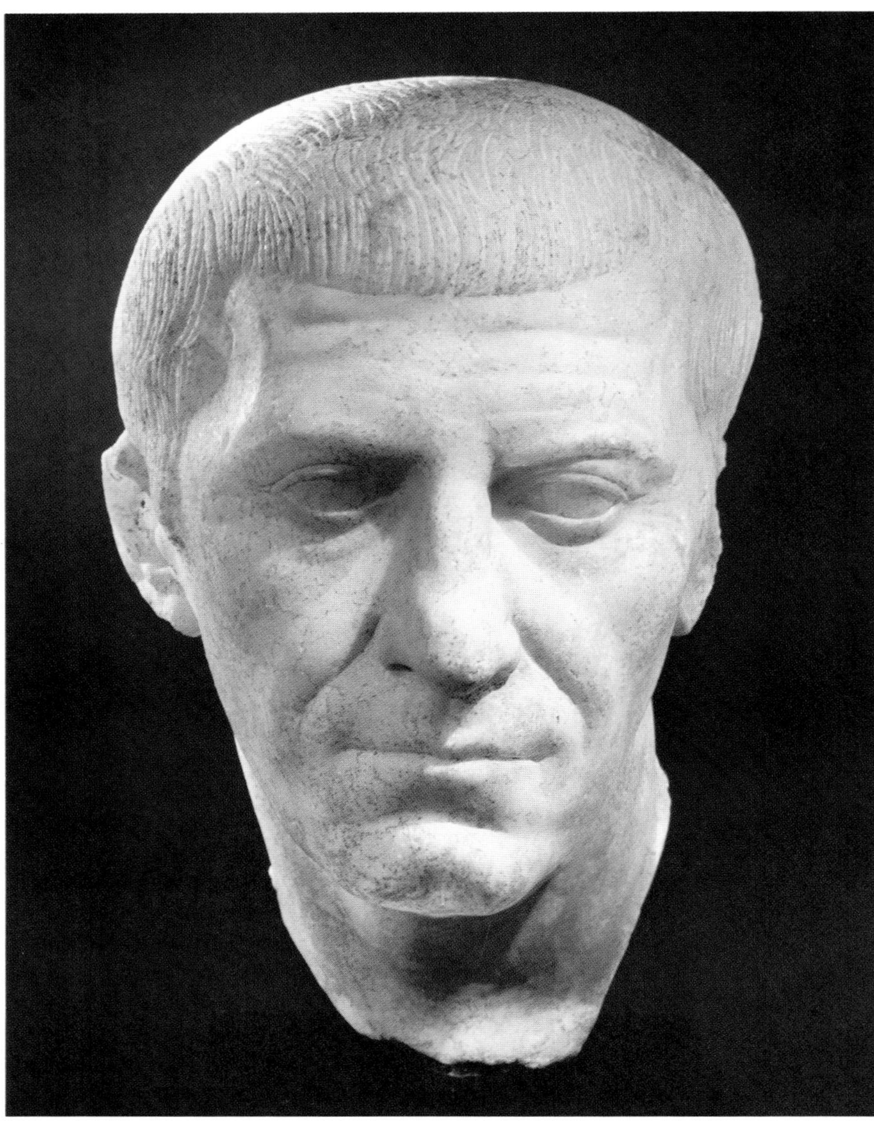

Roman art emerged from the Greek heritage. The Romans imported Greek sculptors to work in Rome and, in fact, made copies of Greek works. Through their colonization of the Mediterranean, they also were able to acquire many Greek works of art. In spite of this dependence, Roman art had its own specific character. The Romans developed an official art which expressed the political power of the Roman state. The Greeks had never developed political iconography in their art. The fine marble portrait head (fig. 27) is a first-century copy of a statue executed during the period when Rome was a republic between 500 and 44 BC. The Romans had gained control over the other peoples living on the Italian peninsula by the end of the fifth century BC. Until then, Italy had been dominated by the Etruscans, a people whose origins can be traced to Asia Minor.

The Museum portrait (fig. 27) probably depicts a government official. In the Early Republican period, from the second to the first century BC, the Romans, under the influence of Etruscan sculpture, made realistic portraits of their ancestors. During the later Republican period in first century BC, the Romans sought to idealize

Fig. 28
Unknown Roman Painter
Landscape Scene
Fragment of a fresco
Pompeian Fourth Style, 60-79 AD
Horsley and Annie Townsend
  Bequest
969.1625

the portrait in order to depict the sitter as a powerful and famous person. The Museum's portrait (fig. 27) is similar in style to the portrait of Julius Caesar in the Vatican Museum, dated 45 BC. In the Museum's portrait head, the sitter's individual features are generalized. The planes of his face are simplified, and the lack of the pupil in the eye prevents the viewer from perceiving the sitter's inner psychological state. By understating the sitter's individual characteristics, the artist reinforces his role as a public figure.

The Romans also made several important advances in the depiction of space in painting. Whereas the Greeks had discovered certain methods of representing linear perspective in a fragmentary way, the Romans went even further and developed atmospheric perspective. A fragment of a fresco (fig. 28) acquired by the Museum in 1969, is representative of fourth style Pompeian painting, current from 60 to 79 AD. It may well have come from the wall of a house near Pompeii. This fragment shows a landscape scene with a temple in the foreground. Part of a frame is still visible above the landscape at the top. In its initial context, this landscape would have represented an illusionistic painting. The artist has opened up the space of the wall, providing an optical illusion of depth through the use of areas of color flooded with light and atmosphere. The background figures are treated as silhouettes, contrasting with those in the foreground which are shown in greater detail. The artist understood that forms become less distinct and colours fade as they recede from the viewer, the fundamental principle of atmospheric perspective.

As you proceed to the Mediaeval, Renaissance and Baroque galleries you will see how Greek and Roman art was a powerful influence on the art of these periods.

The Museum's collection of Mediaeval art was begun in the early years of this century. Consistent acquisition in this field was further enriched by the bequest of Mr. F. Cleveland Morgan of a number of important works of Mediaeval art. Since that time, several significant acquisitions have been made, primarily in the field of sculpture. At the present time, the collection is composed for the most part of works of art from Western Europe, although Byzantine art is represented by several examples.

The Early Christian era, the earliest period of Mediaeval art, begins "officially" with the recognition of Christianity as the state religion of the Roman Empire by the Emperor Constantine in 331 AD and the foundation of the city of Constantinople as the capital of the eastern part of the Roman Empire. In the West, the most important centers of Early Christian art were Ravenna, Milan and Rome. Early Christian art developed from two different heritages. On the one hand, it was influenced by the naturalistic, illusionistic style of Roman painting, as well as the tradition of Roman Imperial portraiture. On the other hand, it quickly adopted the flat, hieratic figural compositions of the contemporary Near Eastern art of Syria, Egypt, Asia Minor and Anatolia which, through the gradual shift in the power of the Roman Empire to the eastern part of the realm, had already begun to influence Late Roman art.

The art of the Mediaeval West continued the tradition of Early Christian art. At the same time, however, another major source of early Mediaeval art was the pagan art of the "barbarians" who overran Europe after the fall of Rome in the fourth and fifth centuries AD. These tribes, such as the Ostrogoths, Visigoths, and Vandals, were essentially nomadic, and thus they did not develop their own tradition of monumental art or architecture. This "Migration art" is limited to the production of small, portable objects, usually jewellery, which often seem to have had a magical as well as an ornamental function.

A tiny bronze fibula or brooch (fig. 29), dating to the Merovingian period (fifth-seventh century) and possibly the work of an Ostrogothic artist, is a characteristic example of Migration art. During the Merovingian period, the nomadic tribes of Europe began to stabilize. Under King Clovis, who reigned from 481 to 511, much of Europe was Christianized and the characteristics of Early Christian art began to merge with those of Migration art. The fibula, however, lacks any reference to religious subject-matter of Early Christian art. It shows that although Christianity was tentatively established in Europe during this period, the nomadic tradition continued as a vital force in art.

The bird motif of the fibula is common in Migration art. The artist has abstracted it into an ornamental image; the features of the bird's profile — beak, wings and tail — have been distorted in favour of a rhythmical shape. The surface of the fibula is decorated with a geometric pattern composed of finely incised ridges, and the eye has been indicated by a cabochon of red glass paste. The piece was originally gilded, and minute traces of silver and gold still can be observed on the raised ridges and outer edges. The fullest flowering of this decorative tendency is to be found in the

Mediaeval Art

manuscript illuminations of early Mediaeval Celtic artists, where the ornamental tradition of the nomads was used to depict Christian subjects.

The major characteristics of Mediaeval art emerged fully during the Carolingian period. King Charlemagne (742-814) united Western Europe into the Holy Roman Empire, and attempted to combine the precepts of the Christian faith with ancient Roman systems of government. For the first time since the collapse of the Roman Empire monumental architecture was produced in Europe. The forms of the Carolingian monastic complexes of Spain, Italy, and Switzerland provided the basis for the later architecture of the Romanesque and Gothic periods, as we know from a plan for an ideal monastery preserved at the library of Saint-Gall. Metalwork, manuscript illumination, and ivory sculpture flourished under Charlemagne's patronage at his capital at Aachen. The ornamental tradition of Migration art and Early Christian art were combined with a

renewed interest in the art of the Roman past. The resulting artistic vocabulary spread quickly throughout Europe, and evidence of its survival occurs frequently in Romanesque and even Gothic art.

During the Romanesque era, at its height in the eleventh and twelfth centuries, monumental architecture flourished in Western Europe. It quickly developed into various regional "schools", interconnected to some extent by the routes used by pilgrims linking the major churches of France and Spain, from Paris to Santiago da Compostela. Monumental stone sculpture was produced during this period for the first time, drawing upon manuscript illumination as a stylistic source. As a result, Romanesque sculpture tends to be two-dimensional and completely integrated into its background surface. Sculpture was used primarily on church façades. It was intended not only to decorate the exterior of the structure, but to teach the principles of the Christian faith to a largely illiterate population. The artistic repertory of Romanesque sculpture was

Fig. 30
Italy, Siena
Romanesque
Crucifix
about 1100
polychrome wood
donated by David Y. Hodgson
965.Df.7

further enriched by contacts between Western Europe and the Byzantine East, established during the Crusades of the eleventh to thirteenth centuries.

Some of the principal characteristics of Romanesque sculpture are embodied in a painted Italian wooden crucifix dating to about 1100 (fig. 30). In the monumental cycles of church sculpture, Romanesque artists depicted Christ triumphant over death in the Last Judgement. Because this crucifix was intended for devotional use, however, the artist has attempted to impress the viewer with Christ's sacrifice on the Cross. The proportions of His shrunken, tortured body are not rendered in a realistic manner. Instead, they are abstracted into a far more eloquent, symbolic expression of the meaning behind the Crucifixion. Like stone sculpture, this crucifixion is two-dimensional, and is intended to be viewed as a picture, not as a sculpture in the round.

A sensitively executed head of Christ, which was originally from a full-length figure (fig. 31), dates to the closing decades of the Romanesque period and, when compared to the Italian crucifix, clearly illustrates the stylistic development of Romanesque sculpture. The elegant, ovoid shape of the head, the subtle modulation of the surface to indicate the bone structure, and the graceful parallel lines of the hair and beard contrast sharply with the more rigid abstract figure of the crucifix (fig. 30). These softer facial features are characteristic of the late Romanesque style in the area of Burgundy in France. The head is especially similar to a well-known group of freestanding figures made to decorate a tomb constructed for the relics of Lazarus, which in 1146 were installed in a church at Autun consecrated in his name. It also resembles some of the sculptures decorating the façade of the abbey church of Saint-Denis, built near Paris in 1137 by Abbot Suger. The sculpture of this church marks the beginning of the Gothic style in European sculpture. In Romanesque sculpture, the physiognomies of figures were made to conform to the wall surface. The figures of Gothic church sculpture, on the other hand, are executed in very high relief and move freely in a spatial context independent of the architectural surface. The head of Christ shows that the influence of Suger's church was making itself felt toward the middle of the twelfth century, and thus it represents the transition between the Romanesque and Gothic styles in French Mediaeval sculpture.

In the Gothic period (twelfth-fourteenth centuries), a profound change occurred in Western European culture and society. The economic structure of Europe, which previously had been based upon a feudal, essentially agrarian society, began to depend upon the newly-important and wealthy towns. At the same time, monasteries began to lose their political and economic prestige, and towns and their cathedrals became the cultural centers of Europe. Archbishops, wealthy burghers, and the nobility emerged as important new patrons of the arts.

Monumental Gothic sculpture cycles, such as those of Chartres, Reims and Bourges, instituted the use of new subject matter, favouring refined, gentle themes such as scenes from the life of the Virgin. Their style is more fluid than that of Romanesque sculpture, and coupled with this "refining" tendency was an increased interest in depicting the visible world. Gothic architecture and stone sculpture flourished under church patronage and metalwork, ivory, sculpture and tapestries were extensively produced for personal use.

Diptychs were used in private devotion and were extremely popular during the Gothic period. An ivory plaque depicting the *Crucifixion* (fig. 32) is dated to about 1325. It was originally the right wing of a diptych, in which two plaques were attached by hinges and could be opened and shut like a book. The representation of the *Crucifixion* in this ivory shows how the intense, rigid forms characterizing earlier epochs were replaced by refined, "humanized" figural types. Christ is sculpted in a graceful S-curve on the cross. The Virgin and Saint John, dressed in garments draped fluidly over their bodies, express their grief with polite, courtly gestures. The pointed arch used to frame this *Crucifixion* is an example of another trend in the decorative arts. Architectural elements were used in this way in stained glass and metalwork as well.

Fig. 32
France
Gothic
Crucifixion
right wing from a diptych
about 1325
ivory
gift of J. W. McConnell
937.Dv.3

Fig. 33
Eastern Europe, probably Greece
Byzantine
Saint Mark the Evangelist
leaf from a manuscript
about 1200
tempera and gold leaf on vellum
purchase
933.1373

It is important to remember that while Mediaeval art was evolving in the West, Byzantine art in Eastern Europe was also flourishing. Byzantine art, like Western Mediaeval art, developed from the Early Christian heritage. Its center was Constantinople, the capital of the powerful Byzantine Empire, and during its height Byzantine art, which flourished until the Turkish conquest of 1453, influenced areas as far west as Venice and as far east as Russia. The Byzantine style is a mixture of Late Roman elements, which were transmitted to the east during the Early Christian period, and the contemporary Near Eastern art of Syria, Egypt, Asia Minor and Anatolia. In a late Byzantine illumination from an evangeliary, probably painted in Greece around 1200 (fig. 33), these two traditions are combined into the distinctive Byzantine style. Saint Mark, who is in the act of composing his gospel, sits at a writing stand. He is dressed in a Roman tunic and toga. These types of "evangelist portraits" are part of a tradition which can be traced through Early Christian art to Roman times. Greek letters inscribe Saint Mark's name on the gold background. As in the Gothic ivory (fig. 32), the scene is framed by an arch, but here it is less substantial. The columns of the arch have not been coloured in, and their transparency gives them a weightless

Fig. 34
England, Nottingham
Trinity
about 1400
alabaster
Horsley and Annie Townsend
 Bequest
955.Dv.1

quality. Decorative foliage derived from eastern prototypes surrounds the arch.

  The Museum collection of Mediaeval art includes a number of works of art dating to the last phases of the Gothic period. Among these, an alabaster *Trinity* (fig. 34) is an extremely late example, dating to the fifteenth century. It was produced in Nottingham (England), an area where newer artistic movements, already current in many other parts of Europe, were slow to make themselves felt. The arrangement of figures in this scene conforms to traditional representations of the *Trinity*, with the Crucified Christ placed directly in front of the en-throned God the Father. A hole in the chest of the figure of God the Father is all that remains of the dove that represented the Holy Spirit. The six kneeling angels act as a frame around the central *Trinity* group. The two on the upper portion of the panel once held censers and the lower ones hold chalices with which to catch the blood of Christ. Their elongated bodies and flowing robes are fully consistent with the Gothic tendency toward the graceful delineation of figures.

However, the figure of the Crucified Christ, with its carefully observed musculature, evokes the human form in a more realistic manner and, therefore, it contrasts sharply with the other figures in the composition. The representations of the Crucifixion in the Italian sculpture (fig. 30), the ivory plaque (fig. 32), and in this alabaster relief outline the changes in the interpretation of this important subject in Mediaeval art, from rigid abstraction, to refined elegance and, finally, to a more anatomically convincing evocation of the human form.

In Western Europe artists of the fourteenth century, influenced by the emergence of humanism, turned to antique sources in an attempt to reintegrate the achievements of the Classical era into their own age. Thus, during the Renaissance, artists abandoned Mediaeval abstraction and sought to represent the world around them. The courtly elegance of the Gothic style, however, lingered in many centers, and for a brief time during the fifteenth century, it was reinterpreted into the "International Gothic" style.

The Renaissance collection of the Montreal Museum includes bronzes, paintings, majolica ware and furniture from Italy, Spain, Germany, France and Flanders. Two of the earliest acquisitions in 1920 were the paintings of *Judith* and *Dido* by a follower of Mantegna. More recent additions include the two panels of *Christ Stripped of His Garments for the Crucifixion* and the *Nailing of Christ to the Cross* by an unknown German painter from Augsburg of about 1500, acquired in 1973.

A profound change occurred in European art around 1300. During the Middle Ages, history was considered to be continuous, with no breaks other than the birth of Christ which divided the Christian from the Pagan era. It was the Italian writer Petrarch who, in 1338 in his poem *Africa*, changed this concept of history. While looking at the ruins of the city of Rome, he lamented its destruction. Petrarch divided history into three periods, the Roman past, the Middle Ages and the contemporary period when Rome would be revived. The word "renaissance" means, in French, rebirth. In painting, sculpture and architecture, we associate two basic elements with the Renaissance: the revival of Roman antiquity and the search for new methods of representing reality. In contrast to the Middle Ages where the artist communicated by abstract symbol, the Renaissance artist strove for expression by presenting the viewer with the illusion of reality before him.

During the fourteenth to sixteenth centuries, Italy consisted of a large number of independent city-states, from the republics of Florence and Venice to the duchy of Milan, each an important art center. The Republic of Florence was one of the most significant of these centers. In fact, in the fourteenth century both Dante and Boccaccio singled out the Florentine painter Giotto (1267-1337) as having transformed the art of his time. We find a reflection of Giotto's innovations in the *Coronation of the Virgin* attributed to the Florentine painter Niccolò di Pietro Gerini (fig. 35), who was active between 1368 and 1416. Gerini probably was a pupil of Taddeo Gaddi, a member of Giotto's workshop. This painting in tempera on wood with a gilded background can be dated about 1390. Originally it was probably the altarpiece of a guild house in Florence, since the Saints Francis of Assisi, Mary Magdalene, Catherine of Alexandria and John the Baptist are included in the same panel with the Coronation of the Virgin. The guilds played a large role in the government of Florence and in the patronage of religious art. In 1367, the Major and Minor Guilds organized a committee to commission a new dome for Florence Cathedral. Gerini, like Giotto, presents the viewer with a supernatural event, the Coronation of the Virgin, but attempts to give this event a concrete appearance. Gerini approximates the scientific method of one-point perspective in the depiction of the baldacchino and dais. The sides of the baldacchino and those of the dais recede into depth to a general area between the Virgin and Christ. Gerini also creates an illusion of reality by depicting the figures as a solid three-dimensional mass. This is apparent in the way in which the Virgin, music-making angels and Christ are placed in three-quarter positions with their legs shown clearly between the drapery. Gerini modulates the folds of the drapery and parts of the body through the use of chiaroscouro.

Fig. 35
attributed to Niccolò di Pietro
  Gerini
active Florence, 1368-1415
Coronation of the Virgin
tempera on wood panel
about 1390
John W. Tempest Bequest
951.1059

Fig. 36
Antonio di Puccio Pisano, called
    Pisanello
born Pisa before 1395 – died
    Rome 1455
Marriage Medal of Leonello d'Este
lead, obverse
1444
gift of F. Cleveland Morgan
957.Dm.3

Fig. 37
Antonio di Puccio Pisano, called
    Pisanello
born Pisa before 1395 – died
    Rome 1455
Marriage Medal of Leonello d'Este
lead, reverse
1444
gift of F. Cleveland Morgan
957.Dm.3

The medal of Leonello d'Este by Pisanello (fig. 36) illustrates clearly the revival of Roman art during the Renaissance. Leonello d'Este was Duke of Ferrara and commissioned this medal in honour of his marriage to Maria of Aragon in 1444. On the reverse of this medal (fig. 37) there is an allegory of this event. Leonello is represented as the lion who is being subdued by Cupid. Behind these figures, we see the eagle, the heraldic emblem of the d'Este family, and the open sail and mast, a symbol of fidelity in marriage. Pisanello was a painter, and he signed his name along with the date in Latin on the reverse of this medal, *opus pisani pictoris,* the work of Pisano, the painter. This is one of the first medals where an artist had imitated Roman coins. The bust of Leonello (fig. 36) in profile with the arms cut off at the shoulders reveals a source in Roman coins. The Latin inscription in which Leonello d'Este is called not only Duke but also King of Ferrara, Reggio and Modena, is also evidence of his desire to trace his ancestry back to the Roman emperors. Leonello's image as a modern ruler has been enhanced by these allusions to Roman antiquity.

Florence flourished under the dominance of the Medici (1434-1492) in the fifteenth century. In art, new scientific methods were developed for the representation of the visual world. This is apparent in the one-point perspective used in the depiction of the tiled floor in the painting *Christ and the Virgin Interceding for Mankind* (fig. 38) attributed to the Florentine artist Gherardo di Giovanni, a member of Ghirlandaio's workshop. The outlines of the tiles of the floor form orthogonals which recede back to a single point located between the Virgin and Christ on the central axis of the painting. L. B. Alberti in his *Treatise on Painting* which was written in 1435 devised a mathematically correct system of one-point perspective which could be used by painters. Earlier, Filippo Brunelleschi, the architect of the dome of Florence Cathedral, devised a method of one-point perspective for architectural drawing. In our painting, Gherardo di Giovanni also has attempted to heighten the illusion of reality by carefully depicting the anatomy of Christ's torso and by including a

Fig. 38
attributed to Gherardo di Giovanni
Florentine, 1445-1497
*Christ and the Virgin Interceding
  for Mankind*
oil and tempera on wood panel
about 1490
John W. Tempest Bequest
953.1084

very detailed bird's-eye view landscape in the background. This
painting is a version of an altarpiece which hung originally in
Florence Cathedral and is now in
the Metropolitan Museum of Art in
New York. Here we see a representation of an event described
in the Saturday Mass of the Virgin.
It was believed in the fifteenth century that Saint Bernard, who is
kneeling at the bottom of the painting, was the author of this mass.

This painting was executed in
tempera and oil on panel, a technique which was introduced into
Florence in the second half of the
fifteenth century under Flemish influence.

In the first part of the sixteenth century during the Pontificate of Julius II (1503-1513), Rome attracted many artists from all over Italy and other parts of Europe. Julius II attempted to rival the Roman emperors in his project for the rebuilding of St. Peter's and the Vatican City. In the early years of his Pontificate, he brought Raphael and Michelangelo from Florence and Bramante from Milan to Rome to carry out his projects. After the sack of Rome in 1526, many of these artists left Rome, and other centers in the north became prominent. Venice was an important art center and trading power in the fifteenth and sixteenth centuries, since it was located on the Adriatic Sea with access to the east. You can see in this collection a *Portrait of a Member of the Foscari Family* by the Venetian painter Jacopo Tintoretto (1518-1594) which can be dated about 1545. The sitter is placed in a three-quarter view and he looks out at the spectator. However, Tintoretto emphasized the play of light and shade on the sitter's face and on the rich brocade of his cloak rather than the sculptural quality of the form. Like Titian before him, he gave the paint surface a tactile quality by the use of thick brushstrokes. Originally, this painting must have been ablaze with colour. Tintoretto created the impression of atmosphere around the sitter. This treatment of light and colour is one of the major characteristics of Venetian art. Venice is located on a lagoon and is completely surrounded by water. Even today, the reflections of the light on the water seem to penetrate the solidity of the buildings along the canals.

Spain had close political and cultural ties with Italy in the sixteenth century, since she controlled Sicily, Naples and much of southern Italy. Domenikos Theotokopoulos, known as El Greco, was a native of Crete, but toward 1560 he came to Venice to receive his training. He was influenced by Tintoretto, as we can see in the *Portrait of a Man of the House of Leiva* (fig. 39). The portrait was executed in oil shortly after 1577, when El Greco arrived in Toledo, the capital of Spain from 1519 to 1556. Like Tintoretto, El Greco gave the paint surface a tactile quality but has changed the interpretation of the sitter. He flattened the three-dimensional form of the body into the picture plane and transformed elements of the anatomy into abstract geometric forms. The head and lace collar have been reduced to two interlocking oval flat shapes. In contrast to Tintoretto, El Greco placed less emphasis on the outer physical appearance of the sitter and more on his inner psychology. He gave the sitter an emotional intensity which evokes a feeling of spirituality and mysticism. This portrait is contemporary with the *Burial of Count Orgaz* by El Greco which was painted for a funerary chapel in the church of Santo Tomé in Toledo in 1586. The expression of spirituality in El Greco's paintings is a reflection of the Counter Reformation. The Jesuit Order was founded by Saint Ignatius of Loyola, a Spaniard, with the purpose of instigating religious devotion amongst the masses in response to the increasing power of the Protestant religion in the sixteenth century.

While many new innovations occurred in southern Europe, the north also was developing in a parallel way. The aims of northern European artists were quite similar to those in the south; Jan van Eyck, like Alberti, attempted to heighten the sensibility of the viewer to the religious painting or secular portrait by placing him before a mirror of nature. Van Eyck,

Fig. 39
Domenikos Theotokopoulos,
  called El Greco
Greek, Crete 1541 – Toledo 1614
Portrait of a Man of the House of
  Leiva
oil on canvas
about 1580
bequest of Miss Adaline Van
  Horne
945.885

in contrast to Alberti, used empirical rather than scientific methods. In the fifteenth century in the north, innovation cannot be measured by the revival of classical antiquity. This did not become a preoccupation until the sixteenth century when large numbers of northern European artists travelled to Italy.

In the fifteenth century, Flanders consisted of a number of commercial urban centers from Dijon and Liege in the eastern part of present-day France, to Ghent, Antwerp and Haarlem in the north.

Fig. 40
Hans Memlinc
Flemish, Mainz 1430 – Bruges
  1494
Portrait of a Young Man
oil on wood panel
about 1480
Horsley and Annie Townsend
  Bequest
William Gilman Cheney Bequest
956.1129

Until the third quarter of the fifteenth century, this area was independent and was ruled by the dukes of Burgundy. In 1477 it became part of the Holy Roman Empire through the marriage of Mary of Burgundy to Maximilian of Austria. These cities in Flanders were centers for the wool trade and linked England to southern Europe. With the marriage of Mary of Burgundy, Bruges became the capital of Flanders. The *Portrait of a Young Man* by Hans Memlinc (fig. 40) is a witness to the importance of Bruges as an art center as well. Memlinc was born near Mainz in Germany, but was active most of his life in Flanders. He probably received his training in the workshop of Rogier van der Weyden. This portrait was executed in oil on panel about 1480. Oil painting was known in Europe during the Middle Ages, but was developed to its greatest potential by Jan van Eyck during the first quarter of the fifteenth century. Oil painting consists of using a medium of linseed oil to bind the pigments of colour to a layer of gesso which is placed on a wood panel. The oil gives the colours a translucent brilliance. The secular portrait, which was distinct from the depiction of donors in religious paintings, was one of the contributions of the International Style. One of the earliest known modern portraits is that of King John II of France of about 1360. The unknown artist of this portrait of King John II was influenced by seals and coins in his choice of the profile view. Jan van Eyck brought about an innovation by showing the sitter in a three-quarter view. This new pose permitted the artist to present a more complete record of the sitter's physical appearance. In the *Portrait of a Young Man* (fig. 40), Memlinc shows the young man almost in a complete frontal view close to the picture plane against a landscape. His left hand is included in the painting; he holds a rolled manuscript page. The figure of the young man dominates the bird's-eye view landscape and Memlinc concentrates on recording the exact details of his appearance. He delights in the depiction of the individual strands of the hair and the folds around the eyelids.

Fig. 41
Tilmann Riemenschneider
German, Heiligenstadt 1460 –
  Würzburg 1531
Saint Sebastian
lindenwood
1510
gift of L. V. Randall and
Horsley and Annie Townsend
  Bequest
1971.6

From the fourteenth to the sixteenth century, Germany was part of the Holy Roman Empire, along with Flanders. In the fifteenth century, many new innovations in the visual arts occurred via Flemish influence. At the same time, the Gothic tradition remained a vital force into the sixteenth century. This is apparent in the lindenwood statue of *Saint Sebastian* by Tilmann Riemenschneider (fig. 41), which can be dated about 1510. The statue was a model which he kept in his studio for other commissions of the same subject. Saint Sebastian is shown tied to a tree in accord with northern tradition. In Italy, Saint Sebastian usually was shown tied to a column. In contrast to the artists we have already discussed, Riemenschneider evokes a feeling of religious devotion in the viewer by creating distortions in the human body. Saint Sebastian's body has been elongated and flattened into an almost completely two-dimensional surface. The features of the face have been stylized to communicate a feeling of pathos. A similar emotional expression is found also in the two panel paintings of *Christ Stripped of His Garments for the Crucifixion* and the *Nailing of Christ to the Cross* by an unknown German artist active in Augsburg at about 1500.

Fig. 42
Unknown Flemish Painter active in
  Antwerp
Triptych: Annunciation, Adoration
  of Shepherds, Flight into Egypt
oil on panel
about 1520
special replacement fund
1975.13

In the sixteenth century, Antwerp was one of the most active commercial centers in Flanders, since it was a major port on the North Sea. It was also a significant art center. Quentin Metsys, Jan Gossaert and Peter Brueghel were the most important painters active in Antwerp during the first half of the sixteenth century. Metsys' art reveals that he knew the work of Leonardo da Vinci, and Gossaert and Brueghel are known to have made trips to Italy — Gossaert in 1509 and Brueghel at least once in 1552. These artists are often called the Antwerp Romanists. Italian influence is apparent in the architectural background of the triptych of the *Adoration* (fig. 42) by an unknown painter active in Antwerp about 1520. This triptych was executed in oil on wood panel. *The Adoration of the Shepherds* is depicted in the central panel and the *Annunciation* and *Flight into Egypt* in the wings. *The Adoration of the Shepherds* (fig. 42) takes place in front of a church. The grotesque ornament on the composite pilasters ultimately is derived from ancient Roman sculpture. Our eclectic artist may have been familiar with Italian Renaissance architecture, as well as Italian fresco decoration. He was certainly influenced by Jan Gossaert who used similar architectural ornament in the *Adoration of the Shepherds* of 1515 in the National Gallery, London. The figures and rustic huts in the background of the central panel recall the paintings of Jerome Bosch. The translucent quality and brilliance of the colours that result from the use of the technique of oil painting are especially apparent in this triptych. Later, in the Baroque period, Antwerp will be important again as the city where Rubens pursued his career; these sixteenth-century artists played a role in the formation of his art.

Renaissance Hosmer-Pillow-Vaughan Collection

Fig. 43
Unknown Venetian Painter
The Crucifixion of Christ
tempera on panel
about 1320
loan, Hosmer-Pillow-Vaughan
   Collection
HPV.69

The Montreal Museum of Fine Arts is fortunate to have on loan the Hosmer-Pillow-Vaughan collection of paintings, sculpture, tapestries and furniture. The collection was begun by Elwood B. Hosmer (1879-1946) in the 1930's and is particularly important for its Italian, Netherlandish, German and Spanish paintings of the Renaissance.

The paintings and sculpture in the Hosmer-Pillow-Vaughan collection give us a panorama of the development of European art from 1300 to 1600. The earliest painting on view is a panel from an altar dossal which was executed around 1320 by an unknown Venetian painter (fig. 43). *The Crucifixion* (fig. 44) occupies the center of the panel accompanied by twenty scenes from the lives of the saints in horizontal registers. This type of composition was common in Italian altarpieces of the fourteenth century. The best known one of this type is the *Maestà* by Duccio, executed for the Cathedral of Siena between 1308 and 1315. The Byzantine elements in style and iconography (fig. 43) permit us to attribute this altar dossal to an unknown contemporary of Paolo Veneziano (active

Fig. 44
Unknown Venetian Painter
The Crucifixion of Christ (detail of an
  altar dossal) (fig. 43)
tempera on panel
about 1320
loan, Hosmer-Pillow-Vaughan
  Collection
HPV.69

1321-1362). Byzantine influence was dominant in Venice well into the fourteenth century because of the trade Venice carried on with Constantinople. An important new iconographic theme, the stigmatization of St. Francis, appears in the lowest register in the second scene from the left. Our artist must have seen in the upper church of Assisi or known through intermediaries the first fresco cycle dedicated to the saint and completed in 1307. Unlike Paolo Veneziano, our artist was not influenced by the Assisi Master's exploration of new methods of representing three-dimensional space. He was much more closely tied to the Byzantine tradition.

Renaissance
Hosmer-Pillow-Vaughan
Collection

Fig. 45
attributed to Bartolommeo Bellano
Paduan, 1436-1496
The Entombment
bronze
about 1480
loan, Hosmer-Pillow-Vaughan
  Collection
HPV.37d

The fifteenth century in Italy is represented by a *Madonna* attributed to the Master of San Miniato, a follower of Fra Filippo Lippi and by an outstanding bronze relief of the *Entombment* attributed to Bartolommeo Bellano (fig. 45). Bellano was a Paduan sculptor who received his training in the workshop of Donatello during the execution of the altar of San Antonio in the Church of the Santo in Padua, between 1446 and 1450. This relief by Bellano (fig. 45) shows the influence of Donatello's marble *Lamentation* on the altar of San Antonio. Like Donatello, Bellano had fashioned the screaming Maries after Bacchic Maenads from Roman sarcophagi to enforce the feeling of pathos in the *Entombment*. The *draperie mouillée* which clings to the bodies of the figures also reveals the influence of Roman sculpture. Bellano probably executed this bronze relief while he was working on a choir screen for the Santo between 1483 and 1488.

There are several Netherlandish and German paintings of the fifteenth and sixteenth centuries in the Hosmer-Pillow-Vaughan collection. The panel of the *Virgo inter Virgines* (fig. 46) is one of the most important in this collection. It probably was executed toward 1470 by a German painter who had studied in the Haarlem studio of Dieric Bouts the Elder (1420-1475). This painting is one of the earliest known representations of the theme of the Holy Kinship, preceding Albert van Ouwater's altarpiece for the Knights of St. John, now in the Rijksmuseum, Amsterdam, and the altarpiece attributed to the Master of 1473 in the Church of S. Maria zur Weise in Soest. The unknown painter of the Hosmer panel has

Fig. 46
Unknown German Painter
active Haarlem and Münster
Virgo inter Virgines
tempera and oil on panel
about 1470
loan, Hosmer-Pillow-Vaughan
  Collection
HPV.1

made several variations on the theme of the Holy Kinship. In the center we see, as usual, the figures of Saint Anne, the Madonna and the Christ Child. To the left is represented the mystical marriage of Saint Agnes, while Saint Catherine is seated to the right with a sword, the symbol of her martyrdom. The figures are placed in an enclosed garden, the *hortus conclusus,* usually associated with the Madonna. While the style of the figures is German, the bird's-eye view landscape beyond the garden wall resembles the landscapes of the Master of the Tiburtine Sibyl, a Netherlandish artist who also studied in the studio of Dieric Bouts the Elder.

Renaissance
Hosmer-Pillow-Vaughan
Collection

Fig. 47
Corneille de Lyon
French, The Hague about 1510-
    Lyons 1574
Portrait of Claude de
    Clermont-Tonnerre, Sieur de Dampierre
tempera and oil on panel
1540-1545
loan, Hosmer-Pillow-Vaughan Collection
HPV.7

The realistic portrait was one of the most significant contributions of Northern Europe during the Renaissance. Two splendid examples in the Hosmer collection are the *Portrait of André Reidmor* attributed to Bartel Bruyn the Elder (Cologne, 1493-1555) and the *Portrait of Claude de Clermont-Tonnerre, Sieur de Dampierre* (fig. 47) by Corneille de Lyon which was in the collection of Horace Walpole at Strawberry Hill. Corneille was born in The Hague but was naturalized as a French citizen in 1547 and spent the rest of his career in Lyons. In 1541 he had been made court painter to the Dauphin, who later became Henri II in 1547. The *Portrait of Claude de Clermont-Tonnerre* is an example of Corneille's early style with its precision of detail, clear colours, and illusionistic shadow around the

frame. Claude de Clermont-
Tonnerre was the son of Antoine
de Clermont for whom Sebastiano
Serlio had built the castle of Ancy-
le-Franc in Burgundy. Claude died
prematurely in 1545 at the Battle
of Montcour. The metal frame,
which appears to be contemporary, must have been added to
the painting after the death of the
sitter, since its symbolism refers
to the themes of death and to the
brevity of life. It is therefore used
as a thematic elaboration of the
portrait, and is an artistic device
derived from contemporary manuscript and book illustrations. The
two putti at the top refer to death.
The one seated next to an hour-
glass holds a flower and rests his
arm on a skull. The other holds a
flaming vessel, the symbol of the
departed soul. To the left is the
figure of Justice; to the right, that
of Charity.

The Baroque collection includes not only paintings but also sculpture, glass, silver and ironwork. The earliest work to enter the collection was the *Woman at a Harpsichord* attributed to the Dutch artist Emanuel de Witte (1617-1692). This was the first Old Master painting acquired by the Montreal Art Association in 1894. The most recent acquisitions in 1975 have been *The Leopards* by Rubens and the *Man Pursued by a Snake* by Nicolas Poussin.

The term Baroque is derived from a Portuguese word *barocco* which refers to irregular pearls. Baroque art was not appreciated until the end of the nineteenth century when Heinrich Wölfflin, the father of modern day art history and the Viennese art historian Aloïs Riegel discovered the basic difference between the Renaissance and Baroque periods. In Italy, there was a significant change in the attitude toward religious subject matter during the reigns of Pope Sixtus V (1585-1590) and Pope Paul V (1605-1621), when the Catholic Church in Rome pursued a vigorous campaign against the Protestant Reformation in the North. The Society of Jesus, one of the first manifestations of the Counter Reformation, had been founded in 1534 by Ignatius Loyola. Following the precepts of Cardinal Carlo Borromeo which were adopted at the last meeting of the Council of Trent in 1563, artists like Michelangelo Merisi da Caravaggio (1573-1610) and Annibale Caracci (1560-1609) made the supernatural religious event an immediate experience for the worshiper. Caravaggio, a northern Italian painter who had come to Rome in 1590, developed a new type of lighting to increase the sense of drama in his religious paintings. His technique consisted of spotlighting the main characters against a dark background. He used this technique for the first time in the *Calling* and *Martyrdom of St. Matthew* in the Contarelli Chapel of the Church of San Luigi dei Francesi in Rome (1599). In reaction to the mannerist painters of the second half of the sixteenth century, Caravaggio went back to the early sixteenth-century fresco cycles of Michelangelo in Rome for the formulation of his monumental, dynamic figure types.

Fig. 48
Valentin de Boulogne
French, Coulommiers 1594 –
   Rome 1632
The Sacrifice of Isaac
oil on canvas
about 1630
gift of Lord Strathcona and Family
927.446

During the reigns of Paul V and Urban VIII (1623-1644), many artists from the north of Europe came to Rome. One of the most important was the French painter Valentin de Boulogne. He arrived about 1612, the same year as his compatriot Simon Vouet. Valentin's patrons were Francesco Barberini, the nephew of Urban VIII, and Cassiano del Pozzo, Francesco's secretary. The Museum owns an important late work of Valentin, the *Sacrifice of Isaac* (fig. 48), which was executed shortly before the artist's death. In this painting, Valentin has been influenced by Caravaggio's use of light. We find a similar dramatic spotlighting of the main figures against a dark landscape, and the same monumental human forms. Valentin concentrates our attention on the dramatic expression on Abraham's face as the flying angel pushes his hand with the knife away from Isaac. Abraham's face is brightly lit; Isaac's is in shadow. However, the composition of this painting is not derived from Caravaggio but can be traced back to Brunelleschi's competition relief for the North Door of Florence Baptistry. Like Caravaggio, Valentin has turned to the art of Michelangelo. His figure of Isaac recalls the *Ignudi,* and the figure of Abraham recalls the figure of God the Father in the scene of *God the Father Creating Adam,* both from the Sistine Ceiling.

Fig. 49
Gerrit van Honthorst
Dutch, Utrecht, 1590-1656, active
    Rome, London
Cavalier and Woman Singing by
    Candlelight
oil on canvas
1623-1624
Horsley and Annie Townsend
    Bequest and Gilman Cheney
    Fund
969.1639

Caravaggio's genre scenes were also an important influence on the Northern artists who came to Rome. Gerrit van Honthorst arrived in Rome about 1612 after he had been an apprentice in the Utrecht studio of Abraham Bloemaert (1564-1651), the painter of the *Harvest Scene* in this collection. Honthorst remained in Rome until 1620. He was given commissions by Cardinal Scipione Borghese, one of Bernini's early supporters and also lived in the house of Cardinal Vincenzo Gustiniani, one of Caravaggio's patrons. The painting *Cavalier and Woman Singing by Candlelight* (fig. 49) was executed in 1523 by Honthorst after his return to Utrecht. It is a variation of the theme of Caravaggio's *Concert of Youths* in the Metropolitan Museum. Now, instead of several musicians, Honthorst depicts a single musician with a woman. These two people are probably actors from a theatrical group. Honthorst develops Caravaggio's light in a more dramatic way by placing its source in a candle hidden behind the book held by the woman. The warm, golden reddish hue of the candlelight indicates a knowledge of the paintings of El Greco. The attire of the young woman may relate the theme of this painting to that of the *Procuress,* another popular genre. Honthorst's painting may be an allegory either of love or of the sense of hearing. In the seventeenth century in Europe, genre scenes often had moral and religious overtones.

Fig. 50
Nicolas Poussin
French, Andelys 1594 – Rome
  1665
Man Pursued by a Snake
oil on canvas
1643-1644
special replacement fund
1975.15

Poussin spent most of his life in Rome, from 1623 until his death, except for a short trip to Paris between 1640 and 1642, where he was called to work for Cardinal Richelieu and Louis XIII. Poussin's major patron in Rome was Cassiano del Pozzo, who owned the Museum's painting *Man Pursued by a Snake* (fig. 50). It probably was executed between 1643 and 1644, after Poussin returned to Rome from Paris. Poussin did a later version of the same theme probably in 1648, *Landscape with a Man Being Killed by a Snake,* now in the National Gallery, London. Poussin was inspired by a text of the Roman writer Pliny describing an event which took place in ancient times. The town of Amyclae, near Naples, was overrun by snakes and the inhabitants, who were Pythagoreans, refused to kill them. We see to the left in the Montreal painting (fig. 50) a man fleeing from a snake, while the figure of Death stands to the right. Behind, in the distance, Poussin depicts the valley near Amyclae surrounded by magnificent mountains. Poussin, who turned to landscape late in his career, was influenced by Annibale Carracci and Domenichino. In this painting, as in the one in London, Poussin has employed an event from Roman history as a means of exploring different states of fear in man. Like his contemporary, the playwright Pierre Corneille, Poussin used the classical past to make a statement about the universal condition of man.

Fig. 51
Peter Paul Rubens
Flemish, Siegen 1577 - Antwerp
  1640
The Leopards
oil and canvas
about 1615
special replacement fund
1975.17

Since 1581, the Netherlands were divided into Catholic Flanders in the south, ruled by the Spanish Hapsburgs, and the Protestant Holland in the north, ruled by the House of Orange. Although they shared a common language and history, both countries had distinct artistic traditions in the seventeenth century. In Flanders, the Catholic Church was an important patron. The personality of Peter Paul Rubens dominated Flemish art of the seventeenth century. Rubens received his training in Antwerp but went to Italy and Spain between 1600 and 1608. On his return to Antwerp he not only directed a large studio, but he also was an envoy to Spain, England and Holland for the Archduchess Isabella of Austria. In addition to his religious and secular paintings, Rubens produced designs for sculpture, architecture, engravings, books and triumphal entries. *The Leopards* (fig. 51) was executed early in Rubens' career, between 1615 and 1618. In this painting Bacchus and a Nymph are depicted with two child-satyrs standing over three leopards described in Ovid's *Metamorphoses* as the animals which pull Bacchus' chariot. Rubens had a vast knowledge of classical literature and art. In fact, this painting is one of three which Rubens exchanged with Sir Dudley Carleton,

Fig. 52
Holland
Baroque
Drinking Cup
Amsterdam
about 1620
silver, partially gilded
special replacement fund
1975.Ds.la,b

the English chargé d'affaires in
The Hague, for a collection of
classical sculpture. Rubens has
chosen this subject from Ovid
to depict the majesty of the wild
beast. The poses of the leopards are actually derived from
drawings Rubens made of the
same animal in three different positions. Although Rubens has been
influenced by the *Bacchanals* of
Titian for his theme, his own artistic genius is apparent in the majesty of the wild leopards and in
the lush colours and textures we
find in this painting.

The United Provinces of
Holland enjoyed great commercial
prosperity during the seventeenth
century as a result of the twelve-
year truce with Spanish Flanders
in 1609 and because of the development of maritime trade.
There was a demand for luxury objects such as the magnificent
silver drinking cup (fig. 52) executed by an artist from Amsterdam. Cultural influences from
Italy are evident in the putto
on the bottom of the bowl. The
base contains three scenes from
the life of Christ. Religious subject
matter persisted in Dutch art in
spite of the fact that the Calvinist
church played practically no role
as a patron of art. Commissions

Fig. 53
Jacob van Ruisdael
Dutch, Haarlem 1629 –
    Amsterdam 1682
Bleaching Grounds near Haarlem
oil on canvas
about 1670
bequest of Miss Adaline Van
    Horne
945.920

came from private individuals, members of the middle class, and from professional organizations. Artists themselves acted as agents. One of the most important contributions of Dutch seventeenth-century art was the genre of landscape. The Museum owns a monumental view of the *Bleaching Grounds near Haarlem* (fig. 53) by Jacob van Ruisdael. Ruisdael was Holland's most creative landscapist. He painted almost every landscape type from marine and river scenes to beaches and mountains. In contrast to the landscapes of Poussin, Ruisdael's have no allusions to the classical past. They are visual documents of contemporary localities. The panorama, which we see in this painting, is a type of landscape with a city view in the distance. This type of landscape is derived from printed views of cities which had been current in Northern art since the sixteenth century in the topography books of Hoefnagel and Braun. We see to the extreme left the ruins of the castle of Kleef, in the center the Cathedral of Saint Bavon and the Town Hall, and to the right the church of Saint Ann. Ruisdael dramatizes the composition by creating a subtle web of diagonal lines which recede toward the stable horizon. The calmness of the bleaching grounds is a contrast to the agitated movement of the billowy clouds in the sky. This is much more than a topographical record of the city; it is a "heroic" portrait of the town of Haarlem, a testimony to its greatness.

Fig. 54
Rembrandt Harmensz. van Rijn
Dutch, Leiden 1606 –
    Amsterdam 1669
Portrait of a Young Woman
oil on canvas
about 1665
bequest of Mrs. R. MacD.
    Paterson
the R. B. Angus collection
949.1006

Of all the Dutch painters of the seventeenth century, none so dominated his contemporaries as did Rembrandt. Like Rubens, he had a vast knowledge of literature, history, mythology and Italian art. He was the master of religious and mythological subject matter, landscape painting and portraiture. Rembrandt also executed prints, as you can see in his etching *Land scape with Boat,* discussed in the Prints and Drawings section of this guide. The *Portrait of a Young Woman* (fig. 54) was executed toward 1665. In this and other portraits Rembrandt was interested primarily in rendering a realistic likeness of the sitter. Rembrandt describes the sitter's outward appearance in order to express his inward spiritual life. The *Portrait of a Young Woman* characterizes

Rembrandt's later style, in which he applied his paint thickly and fragmented his brushstroke in order to render the tactile surface of the skin and rich velvet dress of the woman. He also depicted the variations of light in atmosphere. The whole painting is alive with those reflections, and we feel the presence of this sensitive woman.

Fig. 55
Salvator Rosa
Neapolitan, 1615-1673
active Naples, Rome
Jason Charming the Dragon
oil on canvas
about 1670
donation of Miss Olive Hosmer
960.1251

Rembrandt's greatness was felt not only in the Netherlands but also in Italy. The rose and golden tonality of the light in Salvator Rosa's *Jason Charming the Dragon* (fig. 55) was due to the influence of Rembrandt. Rosa saw a painting by Rembrandt, *Aristotle Contemplating the Bust of Homer,* in the Roman collection of Don Antonio Ruffo da Messina, which Messina had commissioned from Rembrandt in 1654. Rosa executed this painting of Jason (fig. 55) during the last years of his life, between 1660 and 1670. Like Rubens, he has chosen a subject from Ovid's *Metamorphoses* to make a statement about human heroism. In a dramatic rendering of the subject matter, Rosa shows Jason leaning over the dragon, having taken him by surprise. Jason pours a potion over the dragon's head. Rosa has infused a feeling of monumentality in the figure of Jason by referring to figures of victorious soldiers from Roman sarcophagi.

Fig. 56
Giovanni Battista Foggini
Florentine, 1652-1725
Portrait of Cardinal Leopoldo de
   Medici
marble
about 1690
special replacement fund
1975.14

   The Museum owns an
important example of Italian Baroque sculpture, the *Portrait of Cardinal Leopoldo de Medici* (fig. 56)
by Giovanni Battista Foggini.
Foggini was a Florentine by
birth, but went to Rome where he
was a member of Gian Lorenzo
Bernini's workshop between 1669
and 1671. When he returned to
Florence, he was appointed court
sculptor to Cosimo III de Medici in
1687. Foggini was commissioned
by Cosimo III to execute a series
of busts of illustrious members of
the Medici family between 1685
and 1690. The other busts in this
series are found in museums ranging from the Louvre in Paris to the
Victoria and Albert in London.
Foggini executed this bust of Cardinal de Medici after the sitter's
death. The bust can be dated toward 1690. Cardinal Leopoldo de
Medici died in 1675. Influenced by
Bernini's bust of Cardinal Scipione
Borghese (1632), Foggini suc-
ceeds in the depiction of the tactile quality of the silk of the
Cardinal's robe, in spite of the
hard surface of the marble. As in
Rembrandt's *Portrait of a Woman*
(fig. 54) we feel the immediate
presence of this distinguished
man.

The collection of eighteenth-century art is one of the most varied in the Museum, as it includes examples of European sculpture, furniture, and decorative art. The earliest acquisition of eighteenth-century art by the Museum was the purchase in 1905 of the *Portrait of Judge Altamirano of Seville* by Francisco Goya (1746-1828). In 1964 the collection was enriched by the bequest of the Lucile Pillow collection of porcelain. This collection contains outstanding examples of English Chelsea, Worcester, Derby, Lowestoft and Wedgwood porcelain. Purchased at auction in 1973 with the aid of National Museums Canada, the *Portrait of Madame Mercier* by Jean-Baptiste Greuze (1725-1805) was once part of Sir William Van Horne's collection.

Historically, the Rococo period in France opens with the death of Louis XIV in 1715, continues during the reign of Louis XV (1715-1774), Louis XVI (1774-1793), the French Revolution from 1789 to 1799, and ends with the establishment of the Empire by Napoleon in 1804. During the reign of Louis XV (1715-1770) decisive patronage was transferred from the Crown to the members of the aristocracy and upper class in Paris. The corresponding period in England is defined by the reigns of George I (1714-1727), George II (1727-1760) and George III (1760-1820).

The term Rococo is derived from the French word *rocaille* which describes the arabesque and ribbon stucco work adorning the interiors of buildings in the eighteenth century. One of the earliest examples of this new type of decoration is found in the *Salon de l'Oeil de Boeuf* designed by Pierre le Pautre in 1701 at Versailles. This architectural ornament is characterized by a delicacy and lightness of form and by asymmetrical patterning which also has been associated with the style of painting, sculpture and furniture of the period. It is, however, not possible to characterize the entire eighteenth century by the term Rococo. At the same time, we witness the growth of Neo-classicism. At the beginning of the eighteenth century in France, theoreticians such as the Abbé de Cordemoy and, in England, architects like Lord Burlington who initiated the Palladian revival, called for a return to the classical past in order to reform the excesses of Baroque and Rococo art.

The moral overtones of this artistic revival are paralleled in the works of the philosophers Diderot, Rousseau and Voltaire. These theorists called for a return to the simplicity, rationality and conformity to nature which, they believed, characterized classical art. As a result of this desire to return to the past, artists and writers travelled to Greece and Rome to view the ancient ruins. Excavations began in Rome in 1726. The discoveries of Herculaneum (1738), Paestum (1746), and Pompeii (1748) followed. Giovanni Battista Piranesi began to publish engravings of the ruins in Rome in 1748. The Neo-classical movement was international. Between 1760 and 1780, J. L. David, Anton Raphael Meggs, Gavin Hamilton

and Benjamin West were all in Rome. In contrast to the Renaissance and Baroque periods, the notion of antiquity was enlarged to include Greece and Egypt as well as Rome. In 1755 J. Winckelmann wrote the first modern historical study of Greek art, *Reflections on the Imitation of Greek Art in Painting and Sculpture.* It was followed in 1762 by Stuart and Revett's book on the monuments of Athens.

The imitation of Chinese art, or *chinoiserie,* is also important in the eighteenth century. England, France and Holland all had established their own East India companies at the end of the seventeenth century. Textiles, lacquer and porcelain were imported from China. Later, Europeans copied these Chinese artifacts. Meissen, several examples of which are exhibited, made its appearance in 1708, and was the first European imitation of Chinese porcelain ware.

During the eighteenth century, furniture forms an essential part of the panorama of these movements. We can see, for instance, in the armchair by Louis François Mayeux, a reflection of the Rococo style. Mayeux was first registered as a master craftsman

during the reign of Louis XV in 1757. The curved seat rail and legs with floral ornament were influenced by *rocaille* decoration. On the other hand, the three chairs (fig. 57) by Sulpice Brizard are Neo-classical. Brizard was registered in Paris as a master craftsman in 1763 and he was later one of the major suppliers to the court of Louis XVI. This type of *Fauteuil à la reine* with medallion back was meant to be placed against the wall of a room. The straight seat rail with *guilloche* carving and spiral fluted legs are elements derived from classical architecture.

Fig. 58
England
The Four Seasons
Derby Bisque
1785
gift of Mrs. A. Murray Vaughan
1971.Dp.13

The Montreal Museum's collection of porcelain is varied. An English Derby bisque statuette of *The Four Seasons* (fig. 58), dated 1785, epitomizes the delicacy and lightness we ascribe to the Rococo style, particularly in the graceful poses of the figures and in the foliage. In contrast, the matte finish of the Wedgwood vase (fig. 59) in the Pillow collection, dated toward 1825, was meant to be an approximation of Etruscan pottery. Josiah Wedgwood (1730-1795) began to manufacture pottery in 1750 at Burslem, England. After his death, his business was continued by his sons. He employed the sculptor John Flaxman, who had been to Rome, to model figurative ornaments. Wedgwood himself owned

Fig. 59
England, Wedgwood
Vase on drum pedestal
unglazed pottery
Vase 1825; Pedestal 1869
bequest of Lucile Pillow
964.L.P.218

Fig. 59
England, Wedgwood
Vase on drum pedestal
unglazed pottery
Vase 1825; Pedestal 1869
bequest of Lucile Pillow
964.L.P.218

an English translation of the Comte de Caylus' *Recueil d'Antiquités Égyptiennes, Étrusques, Grecques, Romaines et Gauloises* (1752). The reliefs of the sacrifices on the vase were copied from figures on Greek vases, and the rams' heads and garlands from Roman sculpture. A Worcester dish, also in the Pillow collection, dated 1770, is a witness to the importance of *chinoiserie*. The blue underglaze and white floral decoration were executed in imitation of Chinese porcelain.

Fig. 60
Augustin Pajou
French, Paris 1730-1809
Bust of Jean Philippe du Vidal,
   Marquis de Montferrier
terracotta
about 1781
Horsley and Annie Townsend
   Bequest
968.1583

In France, the Rococo style is most clearly represented in the paintings of Antoine Watteau and François Boucher. Watteau was influenced by Rubens and Titian in his use of rich and subtle colours. He also introduced a new theme, *La Fête Galante,* in his painting *L'embarquement de Cythère* in 1717. This theme, a reflection of the life of the aristocracy, is illustrated in a painting by an unknown French artist in the Museum's collection, *The Fête Galante at the Castle of St. Cloud.* The terracotta bust (fig. 60) by Augustin Pajou is equally representative of the Rococo style. Pajou executed it as a model for a marble bust of the Marquis de Montferrier which was commissioned in 1781 at the time of the Marquis' marriage in Paris. Pajou was court sculptor to Louis XVI and executed the reliefs in the Opera at Versailles. The sitter is depicted in a lifelike pose, but Pajou idealized his features under the influence of classical sculpture. He had been to Rome in 1755.

Fig. 61
Thomas Gainsborough
English, Sudbury 1727 – London
1788
Portrait of Mrs. George
Drummond
oil on canvas
about 1780
John W. Tempest Bequest
951.1062

In England, as in France, the most important patrons were members of the aristocracy and mercantile upper class. Thomas Gainsborough began his career as a landscape painter in Bath and later turned primarily to portraiture in London. Like Watteau, Gainsborough was influenced by Dutch painting of the seventeenth century. In the *Portrait of Mrs. George Drummond,* née Martha Harley (fig. 61), Gainsborough reflects several portraits executed by Van Dyck while he was in England between 1632 and 1641 as court painter to Charles I.

Gainsborough painted this portrait in 1780 at the time of the marriage of Martha Harley to George Drummond, whose companion portrait is now in the Ashmolean Museum at Oxford. It is significant that Mrs. Drummond is shown in a landscape setting. One of the major contributions of England to the eighteenth century was the natural garden, a reaction against the formal French garden we find at Versailles. The "English Garden" with its studied, deliberately

Eighteenth-century Art

Fig. 62
Giovanni Antonio Canal, called
  Canaletto
Venetian, 1697-1768
Interior View of St. Mark's, Venice
oil on canvas
about 1760
bequest of Miss Adaline Van
  Horne
945.871

haphazard quality, was a manifestation of the desire to return to nature on the part of contemporary writers like Lord Shaftesbury.

The English travelled to Italy and brought back paintings of the "Grand Tour". The demand for the "vedute" or views of modern buildings and scenery is similar to that for depictions of classical ruins by Piranesi and Pannini.

The Venetian artist Canaletto was patronized by English visitors to Venice. Canaletto himself went to England three times between 1746 and 1756. Usually Canaletto's paintings show exterior views, but the Montreal Museum owns a rare interior view, *The Interior of Saint Mark's, Venice* (fig. 62). We can date this painting toward 1760. Another version of this subject was commissioned by the British Con-

sul John Smith and sold to George III. It now hangs in Windsor Castle. Canaletto used an earlier drawing, since he includes in this painting a banner which was erected in St. Mark's in 1733 for the funeral of Scipione Maffei. Canaletto's early training as a stage designer is reflected in the perspective view of the church which is depicted in detail. Typically Venetian is the luminous quality of the golden atmosphere which pervades the church.

Giovanni Battista Tiepolo, the Venetian contemporary of Canaletto, is the most important representative of the Rococo style in Italy. Tiepolo specialized in large decorative ensembles. Between 1750 and 1753, he executed a series of paintings, *The Four Parts of the World,* to decorate the ceiling and staircase of the Residenz of the Prince Bishop in Wurzburg in Germany. From 1762 to the year of his death, he was court painter in Madrid to Charles III (1716-1788). An early work by Tiepolo, *Apelles Painting the Portrait of Campaspe* (fig. 63), is in the collection of the Museum. This painting can be dated toward 1725;

there is an earlier version in the National Gallery, London. Tiepolo makes use of this theme, drawn from Greek history, to paint a self-portrait. We see to the right his actual studio with two paintings illustrating the theme of the Brazen Serpent. Tiepolo is depicted as the artist Apelles, and his wife is shown as Campaspe, his model. The Greek Emperor Alexander the Great looks on. The impression of delicacy and the luminosity of his colours are hallmarks of Tiepolo's style. At this point in his career, the influence of the Renaissance painter Veronese was decisive.

Eighteenth-century Art

Fig. 64
François Sablet
Swiss, Morges 1745 – Nantes
  1819
Family Portrait in front of Harbour
  of Palermo
oil on canvas
about 1810
special replacement fund
1975.16

Two paintings of this period are a witness to the importance of the development of Neo-classicism. François Sablet was called "The Roman" because of the long time he spent in Rome. Like Jacques Louis David, he was a student of Joseph Vien. Vien is credited with one of the earliest classically-inspired paintings in France, *La Marchande d'Amours* of 1763. Sablet's Neo-classical style is evident in his admirable *Family Portrait* (fig. 64). The members of a family are arranged in a frieze-like composition against the vista of an Italian port. The smooth surface of the paint, the distinct outlines of the figures, and the composition all point to the use by Sablet of Greek and Roman reliefs as a source of inspiration. We are reminded of the same sources used in the design of the Wedgwood vase in the Pillow collection (fig. 59).

The origins of Romanticism are also found in Neo-classicism. Hubert Robert's *Young Girls Dancing around an Obelisk* (fig. 65) is a witness to the admiration for a past epoch which has been idealized. Robert, called "Robert des ruines", was in Rome from 1754 to 1765 and was influenced by both Pannini and Piranesi. In contrast to Piranesi, his interest in antiquity was not archaeological. He interpreted classical monuments

Fig. 65
Hubert Robert
French, Paris 1733-1808
Young Girls Dancing around an
  Obelisk
oil on canvas
1798
bequest of Lady Davis
964.1464

freely, almost in a fanciful way. This painting was executed in 1798 at the moment when Napoleon was preparing his invasion of Egypt. There is a preparatory drawing for this painting in the Yale University Art Gallery. Hubert Robert did not know Egypt firsthand; rather, he was inspired by illustrations in books such as the one by the Comte de Caylus and by several obelisks he had seen in Rome. He takes us to an imaginary Egypt where we see a broken obelisk, several pyramids and a sphinx. Time has no limit; modern musicians are playing on the entablature of the base of the obelisk and contemporary spectators admire the remains of this ancient civilization. These ruins touched the sensibility of Hubert Robert's contemporaries and were decisive for the subsequent development of nineteenth-century art.

The collection of nineteenth-century European art, begun in 1909 through the generous gift of William and Agnes Learmont, has increased considerably since then. It reflects mainly the taste of the first donors for the School of Barbizon, but comprises also works by Corot, Decamps, Fantin-Latour, Lhermitte and Monticelli. The Museum owns numerous Victorian paintings, as well as one of the finest collections of the Hague School in North America.

In the late eighteenth century, the French Revolution was the most outstanding manifestation of a radical change that shattered the political structure of Europe. The various artistic movements of the nineteenth century reflect the political, economic and social changes that spread throughout the countries of this continent. The Romantic movement in art espoused a freedom of expression that was a parallel to political and philosophical liberalism. The nineteenth century witnessed also the sequence of three other major movements: Neo-classicism which had started in the eighteenth century, Realism and Impressionism. One can appreciate these diverse artistic movements when examining the nineteenth-century collection in the Montreal Museum.

Painted toward 1800, the remarkable *Portrait of a Man* (fig. 66) illustrates the continuity of Neo-classicism, one of the revival styles of Romanticism. The precise drawing, the delicate modelling, and the smooth brushwork in the painting reveal the influence of Jacques-Louis David (1748-1825). The simplicity of the modelling and the neutral background confirm the artist's knowledge of classical sculpture. This reference to Roman and Greek sculpture was a way for the painter to emphasize the heroic quality of the portrait. For David, Greek art was much closer to nature than Rococo art which he considered artificial. The Neo-classical tradition continued in the nineteenth century in the works of the sculptor Antonio Canova (1757-1822) and of the painter Jean-Dominique Ingres (1781-1867).

Other artists who were active during and after David's lifetime rejected Neo-classicism. Painters such as Théodore Géricault (1721-1824) and Eugène Delacroix (1798-1863) sought to evoke a new sensibility by affirming the value of personal experience as an expression of the heroic side of human nature. These artists turned to new sources for subject matter: mediaeval legends, historical, poetic and literary themes, and nature. In style, the Romantic painters abandoned those sculptural qualities discussed above in the *Portrait of a Man* and adopted Baroque pictorial devices to dramatize their subjects.

Fig. 66
Unknown French Painter
Portrait of a Man
oil on canvas
about 1800
gift of Miss Mabel Molson
961.1306

The essence of Romantic painting is best illustrated in the genre of landscape. The sources of Romantic landscapes can be found in England. Already during the first quarter of the eighteenth century, English architects like Lord Burlington and poets like Alexander Pope revered the qualities of irregularity and irrationality in the "picturesque garden". Nature was for them a reflection of the human experience. The search for communion with nature was expressed in England by the poets Wordsworth and Shelley and in France by Hugo, Musset and de Nerval. In painting, the landscapes of Constable and Turner were an important influence on the School of Barbizon.

Fig. 67
Richard Parkes Bonington
English, 1802-1828
View of the Coast
oil on canvas
about 1826
Mrs. R. Mac D. Paterson Bequest
The R. B. Angus Collection
949.1012

Richard Parkes Bonington, who was British, spent the greatest part of his brief artistic career in France. During Bonington's lifetime, English landscape painting had a great influence in France. In the Salon of 1824, where Bonington exhibited his works, the pictorial qualities of Constable's *Hay Wain* impressed the young Delacroix very much. As a result, Delacroix modified parts of his *Massacre of Scio*. The painting *View of the Coast* (fig. 67) is a testimony to the appropriateness of Delacroix's compliment to his friend: "Bonington is the most luminous colourist of the English School". In this seascape, the fresh colours and light shadows anticipate the Impressionist movement. The clear sky and water, as well as the light touch of the artist's brushwork, are evidence of his talent as a watercolourist. Thus Bonington, as well as Constable, brought the Romantic landscape to France. Afterwards, Isabey and artists of the School of Barbizon, such as Théodore Rousseau, Daubigny and Diaz, further developed landscape painting. During a recent restoration of *View of the Coast,* the late conservator, Antonio Maranzi, discovered that the initials visible in the lower left corner had been added on top of the varnish and that the real signature of the artist was incised on the boat.

Fig. 68
Jean-Baptiste-Camille Corot
French, 1796-1875
L'Île heureuse
oil on canvas
about 1868
gift of the family of Sir George
  Drummond in memory of Arthur
  Lennox and Captain Guy M.
  Drummond
919.30

Corot, who worked in close association with members of the Barbizon School, brought landscape painting to perfection. *L'Ile heureuse* (fig. 68), painted toward 1864, illustrates the subtle tonalities he introduced in his paintings after 1850 under the influence of photography. This work is the largest of five paintings which he had executed for the entrance hall of his friend Daubigny's house at Auvers-sur-Oise. The subdued colours and the blurred forms give to the scene an aura of mystery and poetry which distinguishes Corot as the most prominent of the Romantic landscapists. In the pendant to this painting, *Don Quixote and Sancho Panza,* now in the Cincinnati Museum of Art, Corot began to include historical and mythological figures to appeal to the official taste of the Salons.

Fig. 69
William-Adolphe Bouguereau
French, 1825-1905
The Crown of Flowers
oil on canvas
1884
gift of R. B. Angus
889.17

The Royal Academy of Painting, founded during the reign of Louis XIV, continued to exert its influence in the nineteenth century through the Salons. The Academy acknowledged the tenets of traditional art theory: expression of the values of contemporary life through reference to classical allegory and precision of technique. The *Crown of Flowers* (fig. 69) by W. A. Bouguereau illustrates the aesthetic approved by the Salon: precision of outline, delicate modelling, and elaborate brushwork.

Fig. 70
Henri-Jean-Théodore
  Fantin-Latour
French, 1836-1904
The Display of Enchantment
oil on canvas
1863
John W. Tempest Bequest
936.658

This painting is probably an allegory of youth. Bouguereau exhibited regularly at the Salons. However, Fantin-Latour's *Display of Enchantment* (fig. 70) was refused by the Salon of 1863. Napoleon III, in order to appease the angered artists, ordered a Salon des Refusés to be held in the same year. The *Display of Enchantment* was exhibited along with the scandalous *Déjeuner sur l'herbe* by Manet and the *Young Girl in White* by Whistler. Fantin-Latour's painting was not well received by the critics. They reproached him for having been inspired by Delacroix, Rubens and Veronese. Fantin had been copying their works at the Louvre for over twelve years to earn a living. In fact, the gamut of pink and gold colours in this painting comes from these masters. His thick brushstrokes and the lack of dark shadows, however, show him to be a forerunner of the Impressionists. Madame Fantin-Latour saw this composition as a theme of pure imagination: "A young fairy tale princess comes down the stairs of a magnificent palace and sees a charming prince with his attendants who offers her precious gifts". However, since Fantin had great admiration for the works of Brahms, Schumann and Wagner, the painting may depict a scene from Wagner's opera *Tristan and Iseult* which was written in 1859. Our painting probably shows Iseult disembarking from the ship to meet King Mark after she had drunk the love potion prepared by her maid. This painting was in the collection of the American painter James McNeill Whistler, a friend of Fantin-Latour.

Toward the second half of the nineteenth century, there was a reaction against Romanticism. This movement is known as Realism. Instigated by the painters Daumier and Courbet, the battle was led by the critic Champfleury in collaboration with writers such as Zola, Flaubert and Balzac. Influenced by the theories of positivism and scientism, the artists and the writers of this movement sought to describe the natural behaviour of people in their own environment, hence the numerous subjects chosen from the life of the lower classes as well as the genre painting portraying contemporary life.

Impressionism was an outgrowth of Realism. Toward 1860, a group of artists began to paint out-of-doors together on the banks of the Seine and the English Channel. The term "Impressionism" was first used in 1874, on the occasion of the first exhibition of Boudin, Monet, Pissarro, Renoir, Sisley, when a journalist ridiculed a landscape by Monet called *Impression, Sunrise.* Like the Realists, the Impressionists chose their subject matter from contemporary life. However, what was new was their lack of political reference and their dispassionate point of view. The Impressionists brought about several revolutionary changes in technique. They

were the first artists to execute their landscapes completely out-of-doors instead of recomposing their paintings in the studio from sketches, as did most of the painters of the Barbizon School. Boudin, who is well represented in the Museum's collection, was one of the first artists to paint out of doors.

The Impressionists destroyed the Renaissance notion of the picture plane as a window. Instead they treated it as a flat surface on which patches of pure colour were juxtaposed. Based on the theory of colours developed by Chevreul, the technique of the Impressionists was characterized by division of tones and by short choppy brushstrokes. Observing the law of optics according to which primary colours are intensified when used side by side, the Impressionists no longer mixed colours on the palette but set them next to each other on the canvas to permit the mixture to be accomplished optically, that is, in the eye of the viewer. The shadows are no longer black but composed of complementary colours. The ephemeral aspects of nature are conveyed by the vibrating effects of light. The radical cutting of the composition and the use of the close-up view reveal the influence of photography and the Japanese wood block print. For the Impressionists, subject matter becomes secondary to the visual sensation felt by the spectator.

It was through the influence of Monet that Sisley turned to Impressionism. In 1873, one year before the first exhibition of the group, which was held in the studio of the photographer Nader, Sisley painted *Autumn, Banks of the Oise* (fig. 71). This painting shows the principal innovation of Impressionism. Using contrasting tones of blue and orange, the artist achieves an impression of light and depth. This landscape illustrates the Impressionists' special interest in water and the play of light on its surface.

Fig. 71
Alfred Sisley
French, 1839-1899
Autumn, Banks of the Oise
oil on canvas
1873
Miss Adaline Van Horne Bequest
945.924

Fig. 72
Hendrik Willem Mesdag
Dutch, 1831-1915
Fishing Boats on the Shore
oil on canvas
about 1876
gift of Mrs. M. G. Williams
962.1384

The School of the Hague, well represented in our collection by Maris and Weissenbruch, was in close contact with the French artists. One of its leaders, W. H. Mesdag, painted *Fishing Boats on the Shore* (fig. 72). In this painting he combines the traditions of his country with those of the School of Barbizon, of which he owned a large collection. As in all his seascapes, Mesdag depicts the foggy skies of Holland by means of a subtle rendering of atmospheric elements which reminds us of Bonington and Isabey.

Fig. 73
Auguste Rodin
French, 1840-1917
The Call to Arms
bronze
1878
purchase, Horsley and Annie
 Townsend Bequest
961.1282

Sculptors, like painters, drew their subject matter from patriotic themes. The last years of the nineteenth century were dominated by Rodin. An expression of strength permeates his *Call to Arms* (fig. 73), a quality he admired in Rude's *Marseillaise* (1833-1836) on the Arch of Triumph. The figure of the Fatherland is inspired by Rude's work, but the wounded soldier recalls the Christ of the Pietà by Michelangelo which Rodin had seen in the Cathedral of Florence in 1875. The sharp contrast between the powerful movement of the winged figure and the frailty of the dying soldier is achieved by a strong and suggestive modelling. The original model of this piece of sculpture was executed in terracotta and was called *La Défense.*

It was rejected by the French government in the competition for a monument to be erected at Courbevoie in commemoration of the Franco-Prussian war. After the death of Rodin in 1920, the Dutch government commissioned a version of *La Défense* which was installed at Verdun as a war memorial.

The earliest contemporary works to enter the collection of the Montreal Museum of Fine Arts were the bronze *Portrait of Lillian Shelley* by Sir Jacob Epstein in 1924 and *La Porte Guillaume à Chartres* by Maurice Utrillo in 1937. In 1968, more than thirty donors contributed to the purchase of Pablo Picasso's still life *Lamp and Cherries.* Recent acquisitions have been Lyonel Feininger's *Yellow Street II* in 1971 and Barbara Hepworth's marble *Helios* in 1974.

The change from representational to abstract art was the main revolution of the twentieth century. Already toward 1880, the Symbolists and the Nabis reacted against the objective point of view of the Impressionists. Artists such as Van Gogh, Gauguin and Redon depicted new subjects which were an expression of their inner experiences: scenes of life from other civilizations, visions from dreams, mythological allusions. In contrast to the Impressionists, the Symbolists felt a dissatisfaction with European civilization. They transformed Impressionist technique as well by using flat areas of pure colour, unrelated to visible reality and the result of a subjective interpretation of nature. The canvas became, according to Maurice Denis, a "flat surface covered with colours." The Symbolists, often under the influence of primitive art, distorted and simplified form. In the decorative arts and architecture, Art Nouveau, with its plantlike formal vocabulary, was a parallel to the rejection of Realism by the Symbolists. It was a protest against the mechanization of mass-produced objects.

The Symbolist ideals were continued by the Fauves. In 1905, at an exhibition at the Salon d'automne, a critic called the painters Henri Matisse, André Derain, and Maurice Vlaminck "wild beasts" (les fauves) because of the shocking quality of their colours. Although they used many subjects cherished by the Impressionists, they did not present the visible world in front of them, but their emotional reactions to it. Expression was conveyed by bold, often arbitrarily chosen colours, linear pattern, and simplification of form. Colour was freed from its traditional role as the description of the local tone of an object and became an end in itself. The Fauves painted together as a group until 1907 when Matisse and Derain went their separate ways.

Henri Matisse was one of the major colourists of the twentieth century. According to Matisse, "Composition is the art of arranging in a decorative manner the various elements at the painter's disposal for the expression of his feelings…" In his early Fauve painting *La desserte rouge* of 1908-09, now in Leningrad,

Fig. 74
Henri Matisse
French, 1869-1954
Woman at a Window
oil on canvas
1922
John W. Tempest Fund
949.1015

Matisse expressed a feeling of serenity through the pervasive quality of the red colour and decorative arabesques used for both the background wallpaper and the foreground tablecloth. Matisse's principles of colour are also well illustrated in the Montreal Museum's painting *Woman at a Window* (fig. 74) which was executed in 1922 in Nice. The theme of the window was the center of his research on the interrelationship between space and the flat two-dimensional picture plane. The window played the role of intermediary between inside and outside space. In *Woman at a Window* (fig. 74), one feels a greater sense of depth than in the earlier painting in Leningrad. The window is placed at an angle to the picture plane, while a woman is seated in the foreground against a patch of wallpaper with paisley decoration. The spatial depth created by the orthogonals of the windowpanes and the vista of the sea prevails over the flatness of the picture plane into which the woman and the patterned wallpaper appear to be compressed.

The choice of the colours of red and brown for the woman's hair is completely arbitrary. A sensation of luminosity is created by the brilliant strokes of warm colours in the foreground and those of blue in the background. Fauvism had an immediate influence on the development of Expressionism elsewhere in Europe, particularly on Knolde and Beckmann in Germany, Ensor in Belgium, and Munch in Norway. Cubism developed slowly after Fauvism and followed the same principles.

Fig. 75
Pablo Ruiz Picasso
Spanish, 1881-1973
active in France
Lamp and Cherries
oil on canvas
1945
gift of friends of the Museum
968.1610

The Cubists under the leadership of Pablo Picasso experimented with new methods of representing the visual world. Between 1905 and 1906 Picasso, under the influence of the paintings of Cézanne and the primitive art of Africa and Oceania, discovered a new way of organizing formal elements so that he could achieve an aesthetic independence from nineteenth-century pictorial realism. In his *Demoiselles d'Avignon* of 1907, his first truly Cubist painting, Picasso abandoned one-point perspective as well as the Renaissance conception of the picture plane as a window. Instead of presenting an object from a single point of view, he viewed it simultaneously from many different points of view. Volumes were reduced to discontinuous planes which were superimposed on the picture plane. In Cubism, the notion of time has been added to that of spatial dimensions, since objects are not seen at one moment but in temporal sequence. Cubism destroyed consistency of image and appearance and contributed to the establishment of abstract art. In the early phase of Cubism, the palette was reduced to tones of grey, brown and blue. Some recognizable details were introduced to make the image legible such as

a pipe, nose or hair. The choice of subject matter was related to the life of the Parisian cafés: portraits of people playing the guitar, still lifes with wine bottles, cigarettes and print from newspapers. In the latter phase of Cubism, actual pieces of newspaper, cardboard and fabric were introduced and lighter colours were used. These paintings are called *collages*.

The art of Picasso went through many phases after his first Cubist period. Although *Lamp and Cherries* (fig. 75) was painted in 1945, its style can be related to the early years of Cubism. In this lively composition, Picasso returns to the principle of simultaneous presentation. The painter observes the lamp, glass, comport and tables from multiple view points. This explains the distortion of the objects. The artist shows the underside as well as the outer side of the base of the lamp and comport. Because of his concern for the integral presentation of the subject matter, he places one table over the other without respect for the requirements of

Fig. 76
Lyonel Feininger
American, 1871-1956
Yellow Street II
oil on canvas
1918
gift of friends of the Museum
1971.35

one-point perspective. The tables appear to be compressed into the picture plane. The variety and strength of Picasso's works have been stressed often. *Lamp and Cherries,* however, stands out by its gay colours which might associate it with the prevalent mood at the time of the Liberation of Paris.

The great influence of Cubism on the other artistic movements of Europe in the twentieth century can be appreciated in Lyonel Feininger's work *Yellow Street II* (fig. 76). Lyonel Feininger was born in the United States, but studied and worked in Germany from 1881 until 1933. Between 1919 and 1933, Feininger was a member of the Bauhaus, a school of architecture and the related arts in Weimar and Dessau. Although the subject matter of *Yellow Street II* (fig. 76) is typical of Expressionism, its style, for

the most part, is Cubist. In 1913 Feininger had painted with the Expressionist group *Der blaue Reiter.* However, on the occasion of a trip to Paris in 1906, he had discovered Cubism which was the answer to his quest for a new type of spatial composition. Cubism taught him how to flatten volumes into two-dimensional planes. In *Yellow Street II* (fig. 76), even the space itself is transformed transparent planes. A strong yellow tonality permeates and unifies the different elements of the composition. This strong tonality, very different from that used by the Cubists, reveals, like the subject matter, the influence of Expressionism.

Fig. 77
Jacques Lipchitz
French, Lithuania 1891 — United
    States 1973
Man with Guitar
bronze cast, 1972
after original, 1920
purchase, Horsley and Annie
    Townsend Bequest
1972.61

Cubism also had an influence on sculpture. The Museum owns a bronze cast of a work executed by Jacques Lipchitz in 1920, *Man with a Guitar* (fig. 77). Lipchitz had come to Paris from Lithuania in 1908 where he became acquainted with the work of Picasso and Braque. As in the last two paintings discussed, Lipchitz has reduced the structure of the man's body to a series of interlocking planes which are organized according to an architectonic structure. Horizontals and verticals are clearly emphasized. For legibility, we still see the man's eye and the peg of the guitar.

Along with Fauvism, Expressionism and Cubism, Surrealism was one of the most important movements of twentieth-century art. Surrealism developed between the two world wars. It grew out of the Dada movement which had been established in New York, Zurich and Barcelona during the years 1916 to 1917. Its ideals were expressed by the French poet André Breton in his *Surrealist Manifesto* published in 1924. The representatives of this movement returned to pictorial realism. However, they sought to express the fantastic, absurb aspect of human experience, particularly the psychic world of the subconscious and of dreams. Salvador Dali was one of the founders of the Surrealist movement. The *Portrait of Maria*

Carbona (fig. 78) was painted in 1925 early in the artist's career, when he had started exhibiting in Madrid and Barcelona. The portrait reflects the influence of Pablo Picasso and the Italian painter Carlo Carra. At this period Picasso himself reverted to classicism. The strong light and bold outline which make the figure stand out against a dark background contribute to a classical and monumental composition. However, the enigmatic eyes of Maria Carbona and the aura of mystery emanating from her whole person are indicative of the imminent changes about to take place in the work of Dali who was to join André Breton and the Surrealists in 1928 in Paris. The fragment of a

Fig. 79
Salvador Dali
Spanish, 1904 -
Still Life, reverse of Fig. 78
oil on mounted cardboard
1924-25
gift of the Ladies' Committee
969.1640

Still Life (fig. 79) at the back of the portrait is the lower right quarter of a painting executed in 1924. According to Dali's archivist, the artist had cut the still life into four parts and painted the *Portrait of Maria Carbona* on one of the sections one year later. The whole still life has been reconstituted through an old photograph.

Although Cubism, Fauvism and Expressionism rejected the basic philosophic tenets of nineteenth-century Realism, the first truly abstract paintings were produced by Wassily Kandinsky (1866-1944). Kandinsky was a Russian who had come to Munich in 1896 and painted with *Der blaue Reiter*. Between 1909 and 1912, Kandinsky wrote his book *Concerning the Spiritual in Art.* According to Kandinsky, the artist should only represent the spiritual, irrational subjective world within him. In contrast to the Surrealists and Expressionists, Kandinsky believed that the visible world could not be a means for the expression of emotion. Kandinsky produced his first abstract painting between 1910 and 1911. In this painting, there are no representational elements, only pure colours, geometric shapes and lines.

Kandinsky's ideas had a formative influence on the development of Abstract Expressionism after World War II. Three

of the most important creators of this movement were Jackson Pollock (1912-1956), Paul-Émile Borduas (1905-1960), and Hans Hofmann. Hofmann was born in Germany and came to the United States in 1933. *High Summer* (fig. 80) by Hans Hofmann is an example of action painting. In this picture the artist has expressed his emotional reaction to summer. Rectangular planes of heavy paint in red, green and blue, and the ensuing violent contrasts create a dynamic effect suggestive of depth. At the same time, these planes are arranged according to an architectonic structure based on a right angle. While recognizing the importance of structure, Hofmann considered colour and texture as his primary means of expression. His influence on younger artists was tremendous. Through his school in New York, and later in Provincetown, he acted as a link between the European tradition and American modern movements.

Conservation is one of the most important responsibilities of a museum and it is particularly crucial where works of art on paper are concerned. Indeed, such works are fragile and sensitive to light and, even in the most favourable conditions such as those provided in the Montreal Museum, they can be exhibited only for short periods of time. For this reason, the Department's exhibitions are rotated periodically. It is to be noted, however, that the stored material is available for study to scholars and specialists by appointment.

Drawings

Drawings from the most important European schools from the Renaissance onwards are represented in the Department. North American, Mexican, as well as Japanese and Chinese artists are also included. The Museum's earliest major acquisition occurred in 1909 with the purchase of Rembrandt's beautiful *Death of Jacob* of circa 1640 with funds from the bequest of William John and Agnes Learmont. A particular impetus was given to the section of drawings between 1965 and 1975 with the acquisition of works by masters such as Penni, Speckaert, Giordano, Klimt, Bonnard, Lipchitz, Graves and Chambers. The Canadian collection is extensive; many artists, including the Inuit, are represented by large groups of their works. Ninety-one drawings by Arthur Lismer were donated by his daughter, Mrs. Philip Bridges, in 1970. Twenty-two of James W. Morrice's sketch books presented by Miss F. Eleanore and Mr. David R. Morrice in 1974 are an important addition to the large collection of his works owned by the Museum. Through the Saidye and Samuel Bronfman fund for the acquisition of contemporary Canadian art, a number of important drawings by Canadian artists under thirty-five years of age were added to the Department's collection.

The splendid series of drawings representing the *Seven Vices* by Hendrick Goltzius were long believed lost until they were purchased by the Museum in 1975. A Dutch draughtsman and engraver of extraordinary virtuosity, Goltzius took up painting only late in his career, in 1600. The seven vices or capital sins, *Pride, Avarice, Wrath* (fig. 81), *Envy, Lust, Gluttony, Sloth,* as depicted by Goltzius, represent a tradition that goes back to the Middle Ages. Each figure is clearly identified by traditional attributes, such as armour and a sword for *Wrath* (fig. 81), and is strongly characterized through its facial expression, pose and gesture. The little crest-like motifs on each side of the niches are also symbols which re-enforce identification of the vice, such as the lion and the bear for *Wrath.* These drawings were executed in 1592, a year after Goltzius' return to Haarlem from Rome where he had seen examples of antique sculptures and paintings of the great Renaissance masters such as Raphael. These influences led Goltzius to abandon his Mannerist style in favour of more naturalistic forms, like many other artists in Italy who contributed to the development of Baroque art. Indeed, in these drawings, we find a clear, sculptural conception of the form. They were executed in pen and brown ink with brown wash and white highlights. The white highlights particularly strengthen the modelling of the figures which seem to emerge from the shadowy niches. The finished aspect of the drawings indicates that the Museum's *Vices* were destined to be used as models for engravings, along with Goltzius' series of the *Seven Virtues* now in Copenhagen. The plates, however, were not worked by Goltzius himself, but by one of his pupils, J. Matham, in 1592-1593. Goltzius was to have a great influence on subsequent engravers of the seventeenth century, including Rembrandt.

Fig. 81
Hendrick Goltzius
Dutch, Mulbrecht 1558 –
  Haarlem 1616
The Seven Vices: Wrath
pen and brush in brown ink
  heightened with white
1592
special replacement fund
Dr.1975.4

Fig. 82
Giovanni Francesco Barbieri
  (called il Guercino)
Bolognese, 1591-1666
Saint Jerome Hears the Trumpet
  of the Last Judgement
pen and brown ink on paper
Horsley and Annie Townsend
  Bequest
Dr.1973.48

Giovanni Francesco Barbieri, better known as Guercino, is one of the outstanding draughtsmen of the Baroque period. He worked mainly in Cento, his native city, and in nearby Bologna, except for a stay in Rome from 1621 to 1623. Among the Guercino drawings owned by the Museum is *Saint Jerome Hears the Trumpet of the Last Judgement* (fig. 82). The pen and brown ink execution is remarkable, particularly in the transparency of the shadow over the torso of the saint. The subject, which illustrates an apocryphal letter attributed to the translator of the Bible, appeared in Flanders in the sixteenth century. It has been suggested that this very finished work is a study in reverse for a painting executed by Guercino in 1641 and now in Rimini. The layout of the drawing is simpler and tighter than in the painting and emphasizes the dramatic quality of the scene. Saint Jerome's attribute, the lion, and the angel blowing the trumpet have disappeared. Placed closer to the picture plane, the saint and the altar acquire a monumental quality. The composition is much more shallow than that of the Rimini painting and the addition of a second steep hill considerably reduces the opening on the horizon. Although a great number of drawings by Guercino are extant overall finished studies for more important compositions are rare. Indeed it is

believed that, as a preparation for his paintings, the artist executed studies and sketches for details. If, then, the Montreal drawing is not a study for the Rimini painting, what can its destination have been? From its highly finished, complete aspect, one may surmise that it was to be used as a model for an engraving or that it was to be seen as a work of art in its own right. This latter type of drawing, however, only appeared in the eighteenth century, although some scholars have suggested that it was already praticed by Guercino. The Montreal drawing thus continues to pose a fascinating problem for research.

Fig. 83
Jean-Auguste-Dominique Ingres
French, 1780-1867
Portrait of Hubert Rohault de
    Fleury
graphite heightened with white
    chalk
1858
special replacement fund
Dr.1975.9

A pupil of David, Jean-Auguste-Dominique Ingres is considered the leader of Neo-classicism in France during the nineteenth century. Although he felt himself to be first and foremost a *peintre d'histoire,* he expressed himself best in his pencil portrait drawings. His production was incredibly abundant; he left us a complete gallery of the people of his time. Ingres' sitters confront the viewer directly. While their physiognomy is exactly depicted, the viewer is given little insight into their psychological being. The Museum acquired in 1975 the *Portrait of Hubert Rohault de Fleury* (fig. 83) executed in graphite with touches of white chalk at the collar and the left cuff.

It has a dedication to Madame Marcotte, maiden name of the sitter's wife. Hubert belonged to a family of architects and was extremely religious. The folder which he is holding probably alludes to his artistic interests. True to Ingres' style, the head is carefully and delicately executed while the body is only sketched in. Dated 1858 by the artist himself, this fine drawing demonstrates that, at seventy-eight years of age, Ingres had lost none of his virtuosity. Modern artists, particularly Picasso, were to show a keen interest in Ingres' drawings.

In the eighteenth century, under the reign of Louis XV, pastel was used extensively and

Fig. 84
Edouard Manet
French, 1832-1883
Head of a Young Woman
pastel on canvas about 1880
presented by the family in
   memory of James Reid Wilson
923.321

brilliantly by French artists in portraiture. There was a revival of pastel by the French Impressionists. Edouard Manet, who contributed to the advent of the Impressionist movement, at this time became interested in this medium. During the last three years of his life, while he was ailing, Manet made extensive use of pastel because it was easy to handle. Noteworthy among the numerous studies which he executed during those years is the Montreal Museum's *Head of a Young Woman* (fig. 84) whom early twentieth-century researchers have identified as a seamstress who worked by the day for Méry Laurent, one of the artist's friends. This is the reason why the pastel has sometimes been referred to as *L'Ouvrière*. She is shown in profile against a neutral background. This drawing exemplifies Manet's very personal style. He neglected the third dimension and, contrary to his Impressionist colleagues, he did not adopt the divisionism of the tones which was one of the most important characteristics of the style of the movement. Indeed, we note that the face of the sitter in the Montreal Museum drawing is essentially reduced to one plane. Manet carefully blended the marks of the chalk in order to obtain a soft, continuous surface. The neck, however, is slightly shaded with subtle greenish-gray gradations. In the hair, the pastel strokes are also

Prints and Drawings

Fig. 85
Jean-Paul Riopelle
Canadian, 1923-
Untitled
watercolour and ink
1955
Horsley & Annie Townsend
  Bequest
962.1375

blended except for a few wisps of hair on the nape of the neck. The transparency of the barely sketched garment is admirably imparted. Manet's portraits are usually curiously devoid of psychological interest. However, the somewhat melancholic expression of the sitter has extraordinary charm. Manet's remarkable pastel portraits link him with his great predecessors of the eighteenth century, Boucher and Fragonard.

The Museum owns an interesting collection of watercolours from various schools and periods. The oldest, smallest and most important are *The Adoration of the Shepherds* and *The Adoration of the Magi* by the seventeenth-century Dutch master Leonhart Bramer. They were presented to the Museum by Mrs. Elizabeth Drey in 1969. Among the contemporary Canadian works is Jean-Paul Riopelle's 1955 watercolour *Untitled* (fig. 85). Born in 1923 and educated in Montréal, Riopelle was a member of the Automatistes, a group of artists and intellectuals formed in 1943 around

Paul-Emile Borduas. By the time their explosive manifesto, the *Refus Global,* was published in 1948, Riopelle had left his native city for Paris, downcast by the hostility of Montrealers to new ideas. Since late 1947, Riopelle has been part of the School of Paris, but every year he spends some time in his native city and province. In Riopelle's watercolour, it is interesting to verify how a particular medium can influence the style and size of a work of art. In his paintings of the same period such as *Autriche* (1954), he uses thick mosaic-like strokes of paint applied with the spatula. The untitled watercolour, however, has inspired Riopelle to evolve a more intimate and delicate style. Like the oil painting, the watercolour relates to Abstract Expressionism or Action Painting but in a more refined form which has been influenced by Far Eastern models. This is particularly apparent in the predominance of the calligraphic black ink signs. Riopelle's use of watercolour is not at all traditional, since he sprays it on in many layers. He thus creates an indefinable, poetic space to which the arrangement of pink, yellow and off-white colours and of black signs lend a vertical rhythm.

Fig. 86
Unknown German Artist
Saint Margaret of Antioch
engraving, dotted manner
second half of the 15th century
Horsley and Annie Townsend
  Bequest
Gr.1971.160

Prints

The Museum's collection of fine prints is representative of most European schools with examples dating as far back as the fifteenth century. The noteworthy Japanese collection includes works from the seventeenth century to our time. The Canadian school is rather comprehensive, especially in the contemporary period. Initiated in 1909 and gradually enlarged, the Museum's collection of fine prints was particularly developed in the sixties and seventies through the acquisition of works by artists such as Claude Lorrain, Tiepolo, Blake, Corot, Ensor, Matisse, Liechtenstein and Gaucher. Albums such as those of *Les Gueux* by Callot and *Othello* by Chassériau, as well as numerous portfolios by contemporary artists were also added to the collection. In this period, the Museum began to acquire books illustrated with prints, such as the Bible, La Fontaine's *Fables* and Gogol's *Dead Souls* illustrated by Chagall, and Gabrielle Roy's *La Petite poule d'eau* ornamented by Lemieux. In 1975, the Montreal Museum initiated its collection of photographs with the acquisition of important portfolios of works of Ansel Adams.

It was only in the fifteenth century, when paper was made in quantity, that printmaking really began in Western Europe. At that time, prints were mostly used as devotional images. One of the earliest prints in the Museum's collections, probably executed in Germany, represents *Saint Margaret of Antioch* (fig. 86). It is a minute example of a process called *dotted* or *manière criblée* which was practiced in northern Europe in the second half of the fifteenth century. The engraving was executed in relief on metal plaques which were fixed to wooden blocks. This is characterized by white dots which in our example decorate the ground, the saint's tunic, and the stylized plants with arabesque foliage. However, the use of the white line is also an important element in this process since it served to indicate the positive parts of the design which usually appear in black. This is seen in the saint's hair, four-star crown and nimbus as well as the plants, the monster's rings, some of the tufts of grass, and in the title of the print, *Margareta.* Because of the disregard for perspective and anatomy, the composition is essentially two-dimensional. In this period prints like this one were coloured by hand in order to resemble miniatures. Saint Margaret of Antioch was extremely popular in the Middle Ages as the patron saint of pregnant women. Her attribute is the dragon which she is supposed to have slain with the handle of the cross. In the Museum print, the dragon, a symbol of evil, is represented curved around the saint's feet.

Prints and Drawings

Fig. 87
Albrecht Dürer
German, 1471-1528
Adam and Eve, The Fall of Man
copperplate engraving
gift of Miss Olive Hosmer
Gr.961.81

One of the most impor-
tant artists active during the Renaissance was Albrecht Dürer.
He brought to Northern art a
feeling for classical beauty, which
was the result of his knowledge
of the art and theory of the Italian
Renaissance. Dürer's achievements in the field of graphic arts
are outstanding. The *Apocalypse*
which he designed and published
in 1498 was a remarkable innovation. It was the first book in which
illustrations did not interrupt the
text but were on a single page
opposite the text. The most important engraving created in 1504
before his second trip to Italy is
Adam and Eve, also known as
The Fall of Man (fig. 87). The Montreal Museum possesses a particularly fine proof of this composition.
Dürer's figures were obviously inspired by two Roman copies of
Greek statues, the *Apollo Belve-
dere* and the *Medici Venus,* which
were in the Vatican Palace in
Rome and in the collection of the
Medici in Florence. Dürer must
have known them through drawings or engravings. His humanistic
preoccupations are seen also in
the use of Latin for the inscription
which is shown on the foreshortened tablet suspended from the
branch held by Adam. The inscrip-

Fig. 88
Rembrandt Harmensz. van Rijn
Dutch, Leiden 1606-Amsterdam 1669
Landscape with a Large Boat
etching and drypoint
1650
special replacement fund
Gr.975.23

tion reads: *Albertus Dürer Faciebat 1504.* The branch represents the Tree of Life in contrast to the forbidden fig tree. The handling of the burin is of exquisite perfection, as can be seen in the modelling of the figures, in the differentiation of direct and reflected light, and in the density of the textures. Just as Dürer was inspired by Italian Renaissance forms and ideas, his prints had a considerable influence in Italy and the rest of Europe.

Unlike many Northern artists such as Goltzius and Rubens who travelled to Italy, Rembrandt never left his native Holland. However, he was well aware of the contributions of the Italian artists of the High Renaissance and was influenced by them. Rembrandt was not only a great painter but the undisputed master of the art of engraving. Noteworthy among his etchings which are owned by the Museum is *Landscape With a Large Boat* (fig. 88) which was acquired in 1975. In spite of its small size, it is an impressive evocation of the low countryside which became one of the most important subjects in Dutch art during the fourth decade of the seventeenth century.

Rembrandt's interest in landscape took place between 1640 and 1655 and reached its peak around 1650, the date of the Museum etching. The latter exemplifies a classicizing trend which had taken place in the artist's work during the 1640's, replacing the Baroque animation of the preceding years. While it revealed the artist's inner mood brought on by tragic experiences, this change also corresponded to a general development of Baroque art in other European countries. In *Landscape With a Large Boat* the recession in depth is lessened by the alternation of horizontal elements: the quay, canal, boat, stretch of meadow and trees. The effect of space and atmosphere and the intimacy of mood are imparted with sensitivity. The place in the etching has not been identified, and this is not surprising, since Rembrandt never felt constrained to topographic accuracy. Rembrandt was rarely satisfied with the image obtained from his plates and often reworked them in order to obtain as many as six states. However, only two states

Fig. 89
Henri de Toulouse-Lautrec
French, 1864-1901
Babylone d'Allemagne
colour lithograph
Gr.964.347

were obtained from the *Landscape With a Large Boat* plate. The Museum sheet, like the one in Amsterdam, is of the second and last state with very few changes from the first one. It is interesting to contrast spontaneous drawings and etchings such as this example with Rembrandt's painted landscapes which are vast and dramatic.

Invented at the beginning of the nineteenth century, lithography received great impetus after 1891, when the importance of the poster as a means of advertising for the theatre, the cabaret and books was exploited to the full. The Post-Impressionist painter Henri de Toulouse-Lautrec was one of the major artists who raised the aesthetic level of the poster. Between 1892 and 1900, he created almost four hundred

Fig. 90
Pablo Ruiz Picasso
Spanish, 1881-1973
The Blind Minotaur
aquatint and etching
about 1935
Horsley and Annie Townsend
  Bequest
Gr.964.348

posters. They are an extraordinary account of Parisian life of the time. He composed directly on the stone. One of the most important examples from Lautrec's lithographic oeuvre, *Babylone d'Allemagne* (fig. 89) is owned by the Museum. It was executed in 1894 to advertise a book written by Victor Joze, the pen name of a Polish writer, Victor Dobrski, one of the artist's friends. Japanese woodcuts were probably the main source of inspiration for the composition, the compression of space, and the curved rhythmic outlines. The very sober gray-green tones of the poster are combined with a few yellow and bright red accents. Toulouse-Lautrec's posters had an immense success and were greatly influential.

Pablo Picasso is one of the greatest artistic personalities of our time. In every field of art — painting, sculpture and engraving — he constantly experimented with new forms and new techniques. His printed oeuvre is one of the most significant of the century. Between 1930 and 1937, the important art dealer and publisher Ambroise Vollard published a series of one hundred prints created by Picasso on various themes. The *Vollard Suite* holds an enormous importance in the engraved oeuvre of Picasso from the point of view of iconography and technique. Eleven of the plates evoke the theme of the Minotaur, a half-animal, half-man freely inspired after the ancient myth. In 1934, a related theme, *The Blind Minotaur* was represented in four compositions which are among the most poignant of the artist's creations. The Montreal Museum owns a print from the last plate of this particular series, *The Blind Minotaur Guided through the Night by a Girl Holding a White Dove* (fig. 90), in which the techniques of aquatint and etching are masterfully combined. Picasso seems to have endowed his tragic hero with the blindness of Oedipus. The little girl, who acts as a guide, recalls Oedipus' own daughter, Antigone. In Picasso's composition, she turns with solicitude toward the Minotaur. She holds a dove, symbol of peace and innocence, which appears elsewhere in Picasso's oeuvre. She resembles Marie-Thérèse, the artist's mistress at the time. Set under a starry sky, the scene is illuminated by a mysterious light, the source of which seems to be the little girl herself. A boy at the left and two fishermen in a boat at the right observe the Minotaur with compassion. In fact, the series on the *Blind Minotaur* can be seen as the forerunner of Picasso's 1937 *Guernica*. The manner in which the Minotaur's head is lifted up toward the sky prefigures the anguished motif of the horse in the later composition.

Fig. 91
Africa, Mali, Dogon
Seated Figure
19th century
wood
Horsley and Annie Townsend
  Bequest
960.F.1

The Montreal Museum's first significant acquisition of African art occurred in 1940, with a donation by Miss Mabel Molson of a bronze mask from the Benin Kingdom of West Africa. In 1975, a collection of 500 examples of African and Oceanic art was given to the Museum. Assembled by Rev. Ernest Gagnon, a Jesuit priest, this collection includes masks, sculpture, arms and ritual instruments.

The term "African art" applies to works created only within a specific area of the continent. It does not include the North, whose affinities lie with the Arabic world, nor does it include Egypt. It encompasses the area bounded by the Sahara Desert on the north, the Kalahari Desert on the south, the Great Lakes of Africa on the east, and the Atlantic Ocean on the west. This area can be subdivided into four sectors: the western Sudan, the western Guinea Coast, Nigeria and Cameroon, and the Congo. These divisions, although geographical, also reflect the dominant culture zones of Africa. As no written records exist, the chronological evolution of African and Oceanic art is difficult to trace.

The region of the western Sudan extends from the bend of the Niger River in the north to the rain forest belt along the Guinea Coast to the south. This savanna area was once the home of the old Ghana empire and the Gao and Mossi kingdoms. Today its poor land is cultivated by agricultural peoples who live in small village groupings. The Dogon and the Bambara of Mali and the Senufo of the northern Ivory Coast, each totalling approximately one million persons, are the most numerous. They are among the leading tribes of Africa in the execution of free-standing sculpture, which generally represents the human figure. Much of their art was produced by the caste of blacksmiths, who fabricated not only tools and weapons, but also carved the wooden masks and figures used extensively in the initiation rites of men's secret societies, festivals celebrating the agricultural cycle, and funeral ceremonies.

Dogon sculpture has been known only for some twenty years, and there is no clear evidence dating any of the known objects earlier than 1800. The Montreal Museum is fortunate to own a cult statue dating from this early period (fig. 91). Carved in the round in hardwood, it depicts a seated figure on a circular throne which is supported in the center by a column and at the rim by four arched pilasters. On these pilasters alternately appear, in caryatid-fashion, a human figure and a crocodile in bas-relief. According to Dogon cosmogony, the earth and the sky are two disks linked at their centers by a tree, the *axis mundi*; this is represented in our work by the seat of the stool, the shallow circular base and the supporting column. The figures placed at the four cardinal points around the disks depict *nommos* or water spirits. Stylistically, this work demonstrates features common to sculpture found in the Bandiagara region, such as the starkness and tautness in the handling of shapes, the accentuation of the vertical in the figure, and a geometrical stylized treatment of detail. The material used is also typical, in that most of these works as we know them have a clean, weathered, light surface which, may once have been painted in bright colours. Although sculptures of this type are frequently hermaphroditic, the Museum's figure is most likely a male, probably a chieftain. It was used in funerary rites, as the Dogon, like many other African peoples, believed that the souls of the dead migrate into such statues, which served as the visual focus through which the family maintained contact with, placated and implored its ancestors. Such figures were kept on family altars and were rarely seen by outsiders.

Africa and Oceania

Fig. 92
Africa, Upper Volta, Bobo
Mask
wood
Collection Ernest Gagnon, gift of
la Compagnie de Jésus
1975.F.143

In the area stretching from San in the Republic of Mali to Bobo Dioulasso in Upper Volta dwell the Bobo, a small culture group of the Gur language sub-family. The Bobo are divided into three groups: the black Bobo (bobo fing), the white Bobo (bobo gbe) and the red Bobo (bobo ule). Masks are their representative works of art; figural sculpture is less apparent. In the execution of these wooden masks, paint is utilized to an extent unusual in the Sudan; the colours used, as in the example which comes to the Museum as part of the Collection Ernest Gagnon (fig. 92), are red, black and sometimes white. As among the neighbouring Bambara and Dogon tribes, the masks are fashioned by smiths. This type of mask is said to personify the village

guardian spirit *Do,* and serves the function of keeping the forces of nature, as well as dangerous spirits, under control at times of vulnerability, as at funerals and at the sowing of the crops. It is vertically oriented, with a tall planklike superstructure decorated with the stylized heads of two birds. Its geometrical construction consists of angular and rounded planes, which are repeated in the pattern of the painted surface.

The Guinea Coast sector comprises a number of culture areas which lie close to the equator: present-day Guinea, Sierra Leone, Liberia, the Ivory Coast, Ghana, Togo and Dahomey. Within this area stone sculpture dated to the sixteenth and seventeenth centuries has been found. Large heads, particularly notable for their detailed facial characteristics, are much less stylized than most African sculpture. Although the Museum owns no examples of this rare work, representative objects from this culture area include carved wooden masks and an extraordinary large standing bird from the Senufo tribes, a Baule ancestral figure and an elephant mask, both nineteenth-century, as well as sculpture by the Ashanti and Mendi tribes.

Nigeria occupies a special position in the art of Africa, for it is the only culture in which one can make an analogy to stylistic developments within European art. The art of Nigeria progresses from archaic, to a classical, and finally to a flamboyant style. This area has yielded the earliest dated African sculptures: terracotta heads and fragments from the early Iron Age Nok culture of northern Nigeria now firmly dated by radiocarbon to the period from about 300 BC onwards. While the political structure of the Sudanese and Guinean tribes was limited mainly to village communities, states possessing high culture, well-organized administration, armies and royal courts developed

within this territory. Patronized by court and aristocracy, art became increasingly secular and religious motifs all but disappeared. The brass and bronze sculptures of the Nigerian city-state of Benin spring from this type of worldly environment. Although considerable contact took place between the tribes of this area and Europeans, present-day theories hold that metal casting is indigenous to Black Africa. According to oral tradition, brass casting was introduced to Benin by the neighbouring Ife in the late thirteenth or early

Africa and Oceania

Fig. 93
Africa, Nigeria, Benin
Figure Holding a Staff
17th century?
bronze
gift of F. Cleveland Morgan
962.F.1

fourteenth century, when the king of Benin requested that an artist be sent from Ife to teach the art of casting by the *cire perdue* method. Benin's contribution to this art can be divided into three stylistic periods. The Ife influence dominated the style of the early brass works of the fourteenth to

mid-sixteenth centuries. The middle or "classical" period extended from 1550 to 1680. The art of Benin was exclusively royal or court art, with guilds of craftsmen working under the direct supervision of the Oba, or king. Bronze plaques, such as the one in the Museum's collection (fig. 93), are among the most impressive examples of this court art and seem to be restricted to the middle period. Contemporary European chronicles recount that these plaques were nailed to the numerous pillars lining the interior courtyard of the Oba's palace. The Museum's plaque depicts the figure of a guard in high relief, thus giving him an enlivened appearance. The high bead collar identifies him as a member of the royal retinue. On either side of the man's head and beside his left foot appear three stylized crocodile heads, also in relief. The four-leaf design adorning the background suggests a date well into the middle period, as early plaques have a background embellished with circular designs. Benin's third artistic period began in 1700 and ended in 1897 with the British Punitive Expedition which sacked the city and looted the capital of its treasures. The corpus of Benin art extant today in Western collections derives almost completely from the bounty acquired during this military operation.

The great wealth of Congolese art is found in the southern savanna belt, stretching east from the mouth of the Congo River. The principal tribal empires of this southern area are the Kongo, Teke, Mbala, Yaka, Pende, Lele, Kuba, Songe, Luba and Chokwe-Lunda. As in the Nigerian kingdoms, a strongly-organized political structure culminated in a thriving material culture in which the arts flourished. From the village level to that of the regional chief, the arts served as the handmaiden of religion and politics. The imposing *Mwaash A Mboy* mask (fig. 94)

Fig. 94
Africa, Central Zaire, Kuba
Mwaash A Mboy Mask
buffalo hide, raffia, cowrie shells
    and beads
Marjorie Caverhill Bequest
1972.F.7

from the Kuba complex of tribes is directly linked to royal power, as it represents a son of Woot, the primal ancestor. Woot married his sister and founded the dynasty. This mask, made of raffia and buffalo hide, can be pulled over the head like a helmet. Almost the entire surface of the mask is covered with dark blue, turquoise, white and red beads. A tall hornlike peak curves forward above the facial area in a fanciful union of unrealistic elements with human and animal features. The Mwaash A Mboy mask often appears as one part of a triangle which also includes the Mboom, a larger helmet-mask with heavy, bulging forehead depicting another son of Woot, and a female mask, Ngaady A Mwaash, the wife of Mwaash A Mboy, desired by Mboom.

Fig. 95
Melanesia, New Guinea,
 Trobriand Islands
Canoe Prow
carved wood and polychrome
Collection Ernest Gagnon, gift of
 la Compagnie de Jésus
1975.Pc.31

Oceania comprises those islands of the South Pacific, including New Guinea and New Zealand, which extend to Hawaii and the Sandwich Islands in the north and the Easter Islands in the east. It is customary to refer to the inner islands as Melanesia and to divide the outer groups into Polynesia in the east and Micronesia in the north. The inhabitants of this vast expanse represent three of the major groups of man: Caucasoid, Negroid and Mongoloid. The great diversity of these cultures is manifested by an almost limitless variety of art forms. The Museum possesses such diverse works as an elaborately carved Maori lintel, a number of tapa cloths from Polynesia and an ancestral skull from New Guinea.

To the east of New Guinea in the Trobriand Islands a distinctive type of sculpture called the Massim Style was developed. It is characterized by a richness of ornamentation consisting of curvilinear elements such as spirals, meanders, circles and arcs, often occurring in combination with human and animal figures. The richly carved canoe prow in the Museum's collection (fig. 95) is a superb example of Trobriand technique and style. A number of long, free curves and spirals are combined with the highly conventionalized "frigate bird" motif most commonly used for canoe carvings. Although the general plan of these pirogue ornaments remains the same, no two of them are exactly alike in composition. The refinement, elegance and delicacy of the Massim carving make it one of the most clearly identifiable styles of Oceania.

The art of Africa and Oceania is primarily religious. As objects of ritual and cult, the works of art on view contributed in a direct manner to the spiritual life of the people of these nations. To us they serve as an indication of their way of life.

Fig. 96
China
Neolithic Period
Urn
Kansu province
Pan-shan stage, about 2000 BC
earthenware, black and red
    pigment decoration
gift of F. Cleveland Morgan
950.51.Dp.43

By far the best represented of the Asian cultures in the collection of the Museum is China. Most of the examples of Chinese art were donated by F. Cleveland Morgan between the years 1917 and 1962. On his death the major part of his collection was bequeathed to the Museum. Owing to the enthusiasm and generosity of Mr. Morgan and others, it is possible to present the current exhibit. In addition to Chinese art, the Museum also has fine examples of Japanese, Korean and Indian art.

China

Of the great cultures of the world, China has enjoyed the longest continuous development, extending from the Neolithic period up to the present day. The first evidence of prehistoric remains in China was discovered by J. G. Andersson in 1921, at the Neolithic settlement at Yang-shao village in Honan province. Andersson subsequently discovered other Neolithic sites in Kansu province in northwestern China, one of the sites of which was the large burial ground at Pan-shan. The decoration of the large well-made urns from Pan-shan such as the one illustrated in figure 96 is characterized by a bold spiraling wave pattern, painted in red and black bands, which encircles the upper part of the vessel. In the east in Shantung province, very thin, black, wheel-thrown pottery was found at Neolithic sites which were once thought to be of a separate culture but which now can be shown to be closely related to sites with painted pottery.

Neolithic developments in the Yellow River Valley laid the foundations for the emergence of Bronze Age civilization in China under the Shang Dynasty (c. 1500-c. 1050 BC). Bronzes were reserved for use by the members of the ruling class for ceremonial purposes. They were given as tokens of enfeoffment with the bestowal of land and title, used in ritual sacrifices, and buried with the dead. They were made in a variety of shapes as containers for food and wine. The ornamental patterns used on Shang bronzes are mainly zoomorphic, and include snake and lizard-like creatures, cicadas, elephants and birds. The predominant motif is the *t'ao-t'ieh,* a fierce animal mask with curling horns. It appears not only in bronze but is carved in jade and other stone, bone, ivory, wood and white pottery. The *ting* or tripod vessel shown here is a cooking vessel (fig. 97). The characters inside have the pictorial quality characteristic of early Chinese writing. Most of the characters which appear on Shang bronzes are indecipherable, but they have been interpreted as names or insignia of clans.

Fig. 98
China
Shang Dynasty
1500-1028 BC
Dagger-Axe
North China
13th — 11th century BC
jade
gift of F. Cleveland Morgan
950.51.Dv.15

the tradition of bronze-casting begun by the Shang. Bronzes of the early Chou Dynasty are similar to those of the Shang in shapes and mode of decoration. In time the motifs became increasingly stylized into curving and intertwined bands and scale patterns. Jade carving was also continued from the Shang. The Chou developed a higher level of skill in grinding and polishing jade with more interest in creating smooth surface textures and bringing out the soft lustrous quality of the stone. The dagger-axe shown in figure 98 is an exquisite example of the early period.

The long struggle for power among the warring states in the late Chou period ended with the founding of the first Chinese empire of the Han Dynasty (206 BC-220 AD). Within the more settled political and social environment, a renewed scholarly effort arose. An attempt was made to reassemble and assess the traditional literary and philosophical texts which had been partially destroyed. At the same time, popular religious beliefs and superstitions became widespread and were systematized under a new cosmology which incorporated astronomy and mythological creatures and spirits of nature. There was an increasing concern for the spiritual world or the afterlife. These themes were commonly depicted in art, painted on pottery and tomb tiles and modeled in clay and bronze. The green lead-glazed hill jar (fig. 99) is one of many representations of the mythical mountain *P'eng-lai-shan,* believed to be the dwelling place of immortals. Large quantities of green lead-glazed pottery were made in the later part of the Han Dynasty for use as *ming-ch'i* or tomb furnishings. Models of houses, watch towers, servants, pets and storage vessels were buried with the dead to provide for his needs in the world beyond.

In the years directly following the conquest of the Shang Dynasty by the Chou people from the northwestern regions of China, the Chou took over territories that were occupied by the Shang and appear to have adopted much of Shang culture. The Chou Dynasty (c. 1049-253 BC) carried on in

Fig. 99
China
Eastern Han Dynasty
25-220 AD
Hill-jar with cover
North China
earthenware, green lead glaze
Adaline Van Horne Bequest
944.Ed.21

From the Six Dynasties period (221-589 AD) to the early T'ang Dynasty, Buddhism was the dominant theme in the art of China. Buddhist images were most frequently represented in stone and bronze sculpture and in wall painting. Techniques and formulas of sculptural and icono-graphic representation brought into China initially via Central Asia were adapted to the Chinese taste and sense of spiritual expression. From China these ideas were transmitted to Korea and Japan. The practice of burying the dead with *ming-ch'i* was continued. In the north, tall figures of soldiers, officials and horses were made. Small green-glazed models of houses and animals were pro-duced in the south and were known as old Yüeh stoneware.

China was reunited under the brief Sui Dynasty (589-618 AD) which was succeeded by the T'ang Dynasty (618-906 AD). The consolidation of the em-pire under the T'ang resulted in what is regarded as the Golden Age of Chinese culture. A burst of creative activity, which had begun in the Sui with the building of palaces and temples in a new grandiose manner, was continued in the T'ang. The wealth of the empire during the T'ang enabled it to carry out the projects which were first formulated in the Sui. Foreign commerce was an impor-tant source of revenue. In the T'ang the borders of China were extended farther than they had been since the Han period, and the court welcomed foreign trad-ers and visitors. The extent of

Fig. 100
China
T'ang Dynasty
618-906 AD
Camel
Tomb figurine
North China
8th century
earthenware, "three colour" glaze
purchase
917.Ed.1

foreign contact can be seen in early T'ang tomb furnishings which are characteristically decorated with a three colour lead-glaze. Foreigners are commonly portrayed among the figurines. High-spirited horses and camels (as in fig. 100) are also favourite subjects.

The artistic achievements of the Sung Dynasty (960-1270 AD) represent a culmination of the cultural developments which preceded it. It is a period of great literary works, mastery of the tech-

Fig. 101
China
Northern Sung Dynasty
960-1127 AD
Northern Celadon Bowl
probably Yao-chou, Shensi
12th century
porcelaneous stoneware,
  mold-impressed designs
purchase
917.Ed.15

Fig. 102
China
Chin Dynasty
1115-1234 AD
Tz'u-chou type Pillow
Yeh-tsu-chen, Han-tan-shih?
13th century
stoneware, painted black on white
  slip
purchase
957.Ed.2

niques of painting and ceramic manufacture, and a mature and restrained aesthetic sensibility. The demand for high quality ceramics in the Imperial Court served as an impetus to the production of ever finer wares. Many kilns flourished around the area of the capital at K'ai-feng during the first half of the dynasty. A very fine example of northern celadon made in this period is the bowl with moulded decoration (fig. 101). Tz'u-chou type ware acquired wide popularity during the Sung. It is frequently decorated with charming incised and painted patterns in black and white, such as the bird on the pillow in figure 102.

Fig. 103
China
Ming Dynasty
1368-1644 AD
Bowl
Ching-te-chen, Kiangsi
Hung-chih 1488-1505
incised porcelain, green enamel
  glaze
gift of F. Cleveland Morgan
949.50.Dp.10

Blue and white porcelain was first produced in the Yüan Dynasty (1280-1368 AD) for export to the Near East. In the Ming Dynasty (1368-1644 AD), it was adapted to Chinese court taste and reached the height of its beauty and refinement. From the second half of the fifteenth century onwards, porcelain was also decorated with delicate coloured enamels laid over the glaze. An exquisite and very rare example in the Museum is a bowl of the Hung-chih period (1488-1505 AD) with dragons painted in green enamel over delicately incised lines (fig. 103). The Ch'ing Dynasty (1644-1911 AD), like the Yüan Dynasty, was a period in which non-Chinese rulers controlled the Chinese empire. It is a long period extending up to modern times. Contact with the Europeans, which had begun in the Ming Dynasty, increased throughout the Ch'ing. The decorative arts of the period show the influence of Western taste in their highly intricate style of ornamentation. Large-scale production of porcelain, textiles and furniture was carried on to satisfy the demands of the European market. Ch'ing craftsmanship reached an unequaled level of technical proficiency.

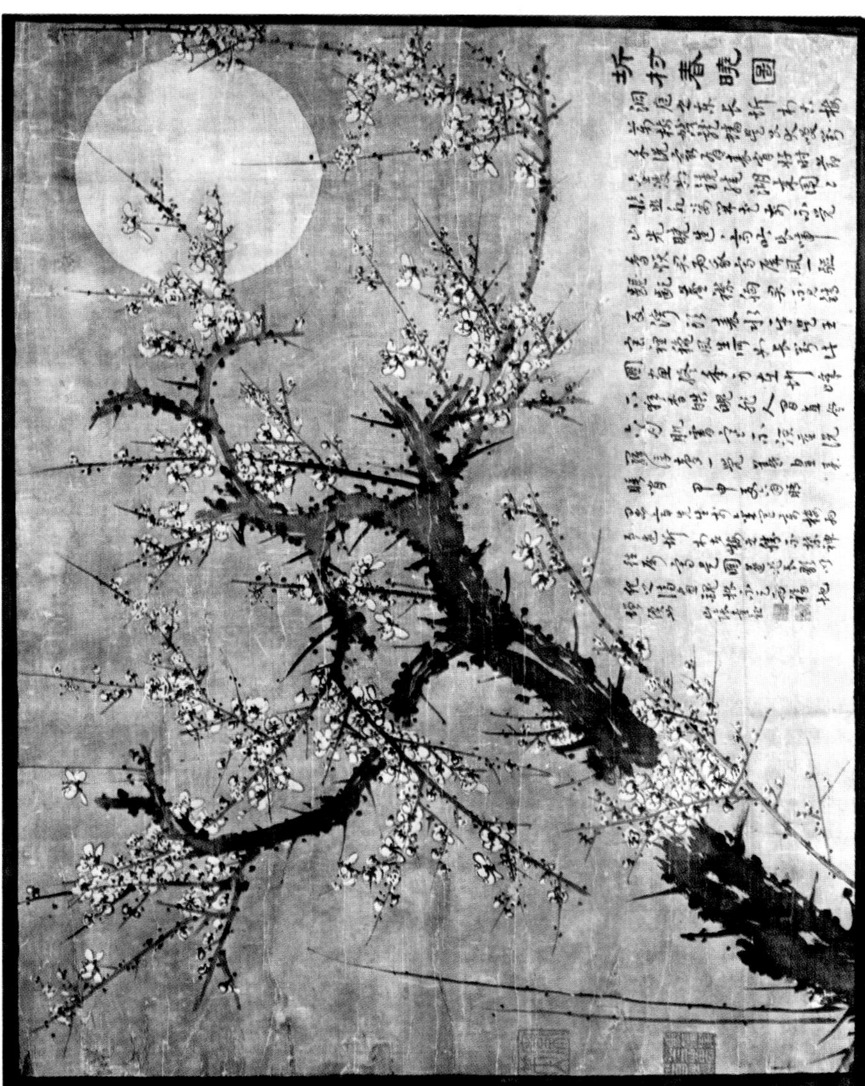

The art of painting was perhaps the least affected by the influx of Western ideas. The Chinese style of painting, which can be traced as far back as the Han Dynasty, is a unique cultural development closely related to Chinese writing. Both calligraphy and painting in China depend on similar techniques of handling the brush to achieve interesting and expressive variations of line. Because the aim of much of Chinese painting has been toward the expression of an aesthetic and poetic ideal with the given techniques of brushwork, rather than the representation of exact likenesses or reconstruction of historical events, it has been the most difficult of Chinese art forms for the Westerner to appreciate. The painting of *prunus* blossoms in the moonlight by Tung Yü exemplifies this linear, calligraphic approach (fig. 104). The large angular branch with its spiky stems silhouetted against the evening moon are the artist's poetic rendering of natural forms. The characters at the bottom include a description of the setting which inspired his work and a dedication to his friend. The work shows the influence of the Yüan Dynasty painter Wang Mien and the Ming painter Liu Shih-ju who specialized in painting *prunus* blossoms.

Painting of the Ch'ing Dynasty springs from the tradition of Chinese *wen-jen* or literati painting which began in the Sung Dynasty. In the Sung the development of an extensive examination system initiated to recruit talented and highly educated men into the government bureaucracy gave rise to a class of scholar-gentlemen. In addition to their official duties, these men devoted themselves to literary and artistic pursuits. The scholarly-gentry class, as well as the examination system which fashioned them, extended through the Ch'ing Dynasty. The paintings produced by the literati were, like the one by Tung Yü (fig. 104), of a very personal, contemplative nature, exchanged among close friends. They are often inscribed with lines of verse or prose by the painter and his friends which allude to literary works or to the paintings of artists of the past.

The building of new ideas with an acute awareness of the past is one of the most striking characteristics of Chinese art since early times. The threads of tradition which run through the highly complex art and culture of China give it its remarkable sense of continuity and progression down through the ages.

Korea

The Korean art collection in the Museum consists of only a few pieces, mainly ceramics. The Korean people are believed to be of Tungusic stock originally from north-central Asia. Due to their geographical proximity to China, they have come under the influence of Chinese culture throughout much of their history. Actual Chinese administration was extended into the Korean peninsula only during the Han Dynasty and lasted up to 313 AD. Tombs of Chinese officials, in the northern part of the country then known as Lo-lang, have yielded excellent specimens of Han style painting, lacquer ware and metalwork. Buddhism was introduced into Korea from China during the Three Kingdoms period (57 BC-667 AD). Of the Three Kingdoms, Silla came to predominate and united Korea under a single rule in 668. The Silla period (668-935 AD) was succeeded by the Koryo Dynasty (918-1392 AD). The Buddhist religion remained strong during this period, under the patronage of the royal house, even after it had declined in influence in China. In addition to fine Buddhist art during this period, Korea produced celadon wares of an extremely high level of beauty and technical perfection which reached a peak in the thirteenth century. Celadons with delicate inlay of white and black clay under the glaze are a unique achievement of the Korean potters.

In the Yi Dynasty (1392-1910 AD) neo-Confucianism became the official state philosophy. Buddhism was banned in the capital and the court. Up to the seventeenth century, close relations were maintained with China under the Ming Dynasty. In the early seventeenth century Japanese and Manchu invasions disrupted the economic and political life of the country and forced Korea to turn inward to its own resources. Blue and white and underglaze red porcelain were manufactured during the Yi Dynasty. The product of the earlier part of the dynasty is more refined, with a delicate style of painting. The later examples, like the charming jar painted in red underglaze in the Museum's collection (fig. 105) are less elegant in appearance, the painting more spontaneous and often with a humourous touch.

Japan

The prehistoric era in Japan corresponds, essentially, to the period before the introduction of Buddhism. The Japanese Neolithic culture, which extended up to the last centuries before Christ, created elaborate cord-marked pottery over several millennia. After the Neolithic was a brief bronze-making culture which left behind large bronze bells cast with low relief line drawings. The use of iron brought about the rise of great chieftains or the earliest emperors whose remains were buried in keyhole-shaped tumuli. On top of these burial mounds rows of large clay figurines called Haniwa were found. Buddhism reached Japan from Korea in 552 AD and spread rapidly. The building of many temples created a demand for images, painting and religious trappings which at first were imported or copied from Korea and China. Soon, however, skilled Japanese craftsmen were

Fig. 106
Japan
Kamakura Period
1185-1334 AD
Kumano Honjibutsu Mandala
Kumano, Wakayama Prefecture
14th century
painting, ink, colour and gold on
    silk
purchase
959.Ee.2

producing Buddhist icons of a distinctly Japanese character. After the Nara Period (710-784 AD), the art of which is strongly influenced by that of T'ang China, the capital was moved to Kyoto where, during the Heian period, there was a flowering of Japanese art. A highly elegant and decorative native style of painting known as *Yamato-e* emerged which was used to illuminate Buddhist sutras and to illustrate secular subjects such as the *Tale of Genji.*

In the Kamakura period (1185-1392 AD) power was held by a military government and the administrative center of the country was shifted to Kamakura, south of Tokyo. The vigorous and lively art of the period is expressive of this martial spirit. The magnificent Kumano Honjibutsu Mandala (fig. 106) dates from this period. It depicts the Amida Buddha in the center of a lotus with eight Buddhas and bodhisattvas in the petals around him. A similar piece can be seen in the Kozan-ji, Kyoto. The Buddhist deities represented are the patron deities of each of the sanctuaries within the shrine complex at Kumano. Erected originally in reverence to the spirit of an impressive waterfall, it, like many other centers of popular Shintoism, gradually became infiltrated with Buddhist iconography. In the thirteenth century the Buddhist priest Ippen experienced at the Kumano shrine the revelation that salvation was available to any who would speak words of praise to Amida. Thereafter the shrine was frequently visited by Buddhist pilgrims.

Shintoism, the native religion of Japan, is originally based on the worship of spirits of nature which have no visible form. With the spread of the Buddhist religion, Japanese artists adopted the representational art and even the gods of Buddhism. Strong syncretic tendencies also can be seen in Buddhist art. Shinto gods were incorporated into Buddhist pantheons, especially during the earlier period of the popularization of Buddhism in Japan. The Zen sect of Buddhism became popular and in the Muromachi period (1334-1573 AD) was a strong influence in the arts. This influence can be seen in the simplicity of design of implements used in the tea ceremony. A sudden interest in the Chinese style of ink painting also can be at least partially attributed to the Zen taste for bold, spare monochrome painting to illustrate an idea or to present a rough portrait of a monk or a priest.

The Momoyama period (1568-1615 AD) saw a revival of the traditional *Yamato-e* style of painting. The men who had come to power in this period were warlords, and their inclination in the furnishing of their new castles tended toward the boldly decorative and lavishly gilded. Screen painting in strong, thick colours, against a ground of gold leaf was the fashion. Lacquer ware, ceramics and textiles of this period are equally brilliant and finely crafted. Painting of large screens continued into the Edo period (1615-1867 AD) using both the polychrome gilded and monochrome ink styles. The art of the Edo period can be divided into three types; the literary school, the court or official schools and popular, commercial art, *Ukiyo-e.* The last of these is best known and represented through its polychrome wood-block prints of subject matter derived from the lively entertainment quarters of the capital.

Fig. 107
India
Chola Period
about 850-1279 AD
Visnu the Preserver
South India
12th — 13th century
grey granite
Mrs. Marguerite Yuile Watson
  Bequest
965.Eb.1

India

The Museum holds a few examples of Indian sculpture, the finest of which is a large stone image from the Chola period (ca. 850-1279 AD) in southern India (fig. 107). It represents the Hindu god Visnu dressed in prince-ly attire and holding two of his attributes, the wheel and the conch. The fly whisks and the canopy above him are the signs of a king. The piece is probably a fragment from a stone temple.

Hinduism is one of the oldest philosophical and religious systems in the world. It encom-passes a large number of deities which personify natural forces. Worship of a trinity of the major deities Brahma (the Creator), Visnu (the Preserver), and Siva (the Destroyer) had begun by the first century AD. The origins of these individual gods, however, can be traced back much earlier to Aryan and Dravidian proto-types. In later Hinduism temples generally are dedicated to either Visnu or Siva. Hinduism was over-shadowed for several centuries by Buddhism, but never died out. Buddhism originated in India in the seventh century BC with the teachings of the historical Buddha, Sakyamuni. It developed into a metaphysical system with a large pantheon of deities not unlike Hin-duism and became the chief reli-gion of India and of eastern Asia. By the seventh century, Buddhism had lost its influence in India ex-cept for a localized form known as Tantrism. A revival of Hinduism occurred in South India and gradually supplanted Buddhism. It initiated a period of great activity in temple building, producing many monumental sanctuaries in stone covered with sculptures of Hindu gods and heroes which are among the most impressive stone structures in the world.

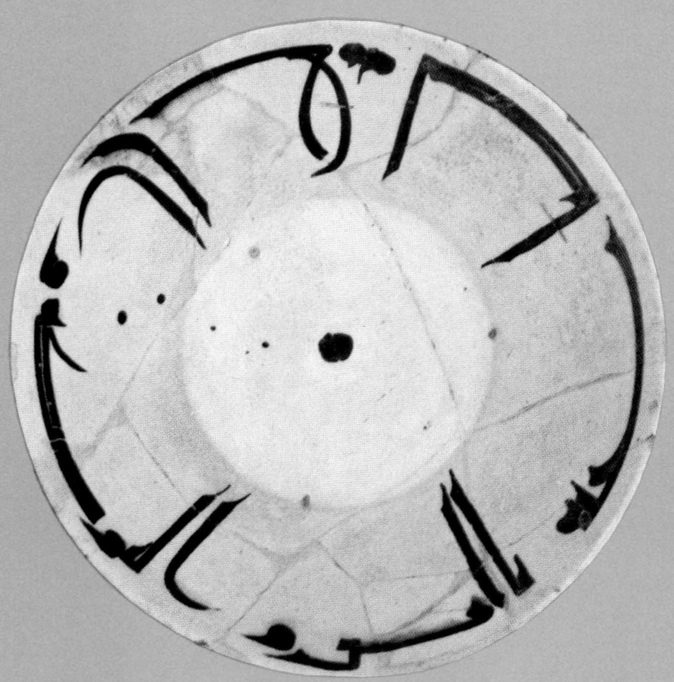

The designation "Islamic Art" does not refer to art of the religion of Islam but to the culture in which the ruling element and the majority of the population professed the faith of Islam. It is comparable to the terms "Gothic" and "Baroque" which signify cultural moments in the history of civilization.

Islamic art was created in the gigantic area covered by the Muslim conquest and extending from Morocco and Spain in the west to India and Central Asia in the east over a period of a thousand years. Chronologically, it covers the period from 700 AD to the eighteenth and nineteenth centuries when Western modes of artistic creation greatly influenced and changed the local arts and crafts. Islamic art can be studied in terms of a first classical period (from the eighth to mid-eleventh century) followed by a second classical period (during the twelfth and thirteenth centuries) after which the various parts of the Muslim world develop their own regional styles and variations.

One of the main characteristics of Islamic art during its early stages and one of its identifying features is the use of the Arabic script as a decorative and iconographic motif. By transcribing the words of the Koran (the Holy Book of Islam), Arabic writing becomes the vehicle of the Divine Message and a unifying as well as identifying factor in Islamic art. Calligraphy becomes an artform in itself and a hallmark of the Muslim world. Up to the eleventh century, the angular "kufic" script dominates all styles of writing. The earliest Korans executed in Mesopotamia during the ninth and tenth centuries are written in bold kufic with brown ink on parchment, as seen in the two leaves on display. But calligraphy is by no means restricted to the art of the book. On coins and in religious buildings, the Arabic script carrying the profession of the Faith and Koranic passages replaces all iconographic and human representations, and on various objects the written word is often the sole decorative element.

The textiles woven during this time often carry a band of kufic inscription woven in silk on a ground of undyed linen cloth.

Fig. 108
Egypt
Abbasid Period
750-1258 AD
Tiraz textile fragment
10th century
purchase, D. W. Parker Fund
952.Dt.2

Known as *tiraz*, such inscribed textiles serve in helping us to date and place the objects on which they appear. They usually carry the name and place of manufacture as well as the name and titles of the ruler under whose reign they were produced. The textile fragment illustrated (fig. 108) with its two lines of kufic inscription on either side of an animal band is a good example of the fine textiles woven for the Abbasid court at the Royal Factory of Fustat (Egypt). By its simplicity and precision the inscription is typical of the earlier textiles produced from the eighth to the eleventh century, after which time the inscriptions become more elaborate and more repetitive.

Fig. 109
Persia, Nishapur
Samanid Period
874-1001 AD
Ceramic bowl
10th century
gift of F. Cleveland Morgan
950.51.Dp.20

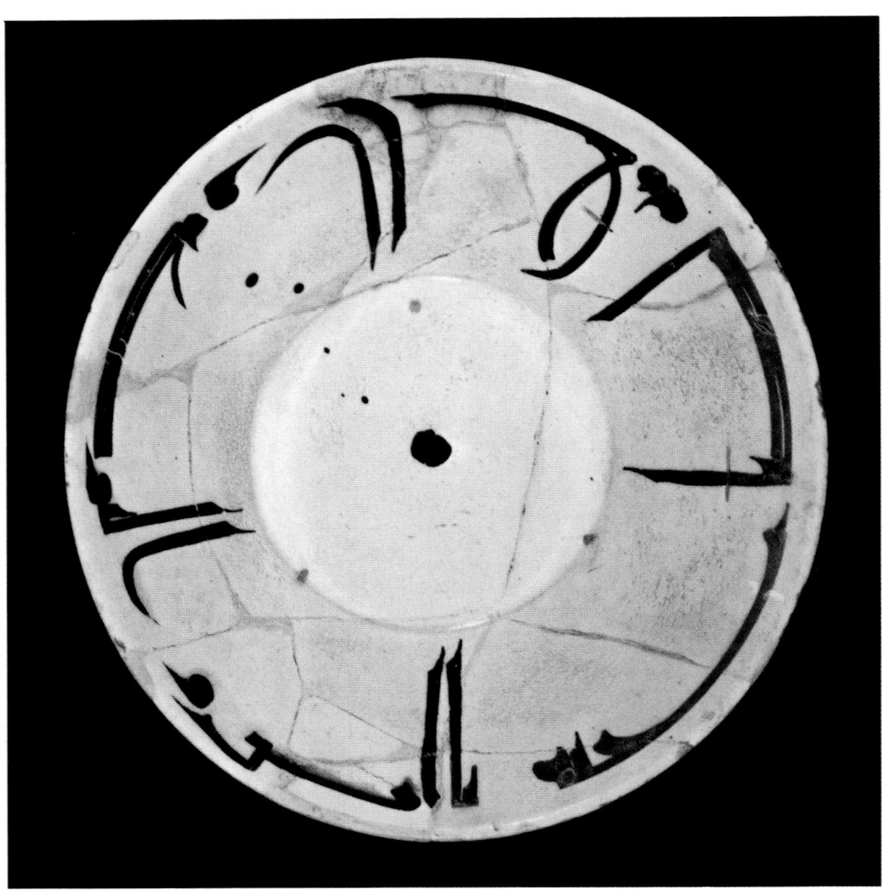

In the field of ceramics, the bowls and plates produced at the main centers of Nishapur and Samarqand in northeastern Iran during Samanid rule (819-1005 AD) also draw on epigraphy as a main source of decoration. These are simply decorated objects with a line or two of bold rhythmic Arabic inscriptions in dark brown slip on a body of white engobe carrying messages of good wishes, popular sayings and proverbs. A very fine example of such Samanid bowls (fig. 109) bears the message: "Joy, Blessing and Peace to the Owner". In the same technique and with the same aesthetic taste, birds occasionally replace calligraphy as abstract messages of good wishes and prosperity. Of the three bowls on exhibition, the bird with floriated wings is one of the finest and the most expressive achievements of the period.

Fig. 110
Persia
Seljuq Period
1037-1300 AD
Ceramic bottle
lustreware
12th-13th century
gift of Harry A. Norton
939.Dp.8

The simplicity of the first period with its inclination to draw on the Arabic script for its decorative vocabulary was replaced in the second classical period by a complexity of forms and designs. A multiplicity of shapes and a wide range of human and animal motifs are characteristic of the Seljuq period during the twelfth and thirteenth centuries. New techniques are developed in the different media to allow an ever greater "animation" of the objects. In ceramics, potters excel in the creation of new modes of representation, especially in Iran at the two main centers of Rayy and Kashan. Techniques such as incising, raising and molding decoration flourish under monochrome or polychrome glazes, and the two more expensive techniques of lustre-painting (fig. 110) and *minai*-painting ("enamel") reach degrees of perfection with results of precision and complexity very much akin to miniature painting. The same phenomenon is seen also on the metalwork produced in

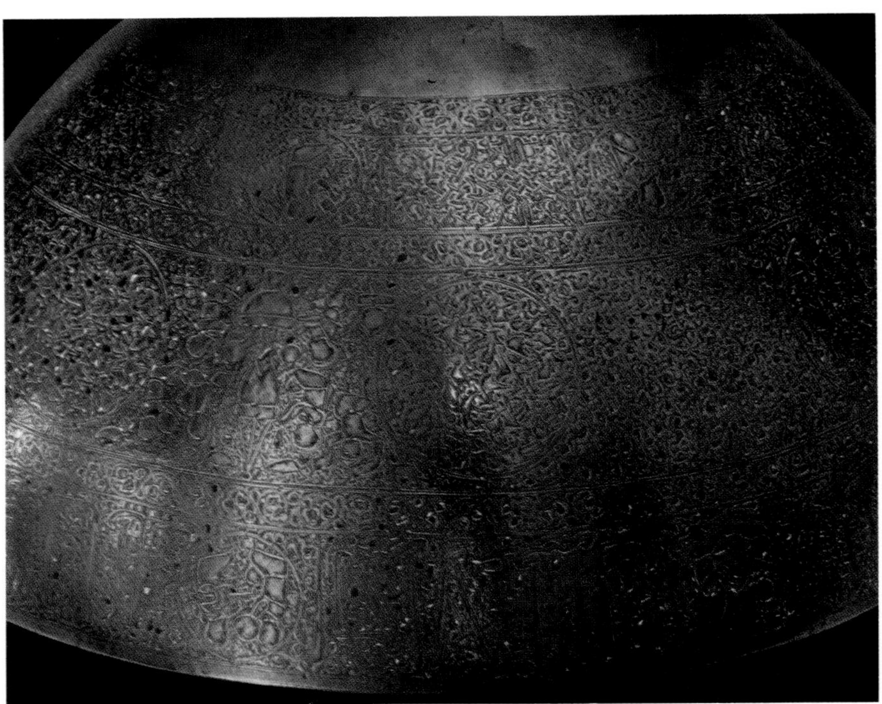

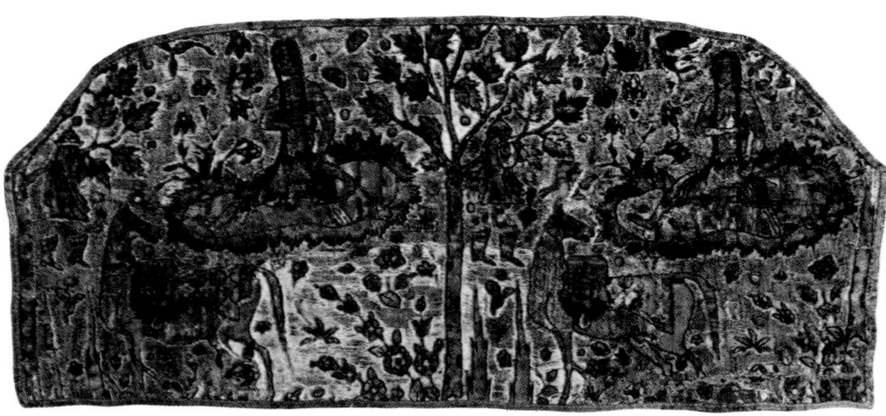

Iran and Syria where techniques of engraving and inlay allow a whole invasion of living creatures as decorative motifs. The semi-globular brass bowl (fig. 111) made in Syria for Salah-al Din-Yusuf, the Ayyubid Sultan of Aleppo and Damascus (1236-1260 AD), exhibits the whole repertoire of decorative themes characteristic of the period. It carries representations from the royal cycle such as enthronement and hunting scenes, as well as activities from daily life such as the occupation of the six figures with a filtering device (fig. 111) on the usual background of stylized vegetal and geometric motifs.

In the twelfth and thirteenth centuries the subjects drawn from life were not limited to surface decoration but also lent their shapes to the objects themselves. In metalwork and in ceramics, Iran was renowned for the production of utilitarian vessels in animal forms. This is represented in the collection by the two thirteenth-century ceramic ewers shaped with rooster heads and beaks for spouts. In Mesopotamia, the ceramic center of Raqqah was known for the production of household furniture, usually molded and turquoise glazed, such as the hexagonal table and the mosque lamp on display. Another innovation of the Seljuq period is the use of glazed tiles for wall revetments. Hexagonal and four pointed units of ceramics were individually executed and decorated and then applied as surface decoration to walls. The four tiles on exhibition are typical of the period in their size, shape and decoration.

With the Mongol invasion, and the fall of the Seljuqs, the shaky unity of the Muslim world was broken up and the different geographic areas had their own developments with independent styles and techniques. Persia, Turkey, the Fertile Crescent, India and Spain produced works of art that can best be understood against their local backgrounds.

In Iran, during the Safavid period (1502-1732), and especially during the reigns of Shah Tahmasp and Shah 'Abbas, there was a period of prosperity and great flourishing in the arts. Although no new techniques were invented, a new perfection and refinement was reached in all the existing arts. In ceramics, glass and metalwork, new elegant shapes developed based on known techniques, and miniature painting carries the developments of Timurid painting to a remarkable degree of delicacy. Of the courtly arts, the textile production, of which the Museum owns considerable examples, shows an unprecedented variety of materials, techniques and patterns. Silks and brocades with floral and animal motifs in polychrome or gold threads are produced in large quantities for an increasingly demanding clientele, and some finer wares such as the velvet fragment from a sixteenth-century tent (fig.

112), often carry illustrations from popular or epic poetry. Our fragment depicts a well-known scene from a poem by Firdawsi where Khusraw's horse stands by Shirin bathing. Finally, a characteristic feature of the artistic developments in later Persian arts is the extensive use of lacquer. The Museum door panels executed for the Safavid court in the seventeenth century represent an early and fine specimen of this technique which was to become very popular in the eighteenth and nineteenth centuries especially in the production of pen boxes and book bindings.

In Turkey, during the Ottoman period, the sixteenth and seventeenth centuries witnessed the development and flourishing of a unified imperial style with Istanbul as its cultural and artistic center. A new decorative style develops, relying heavily on naturalistic floral compositions mixed with the local arabesques and imported Chinese motifs such as the lotus flower and stylized cloud and wave scrolls. This exuberance of flowers is characteristic of all media but can best be seen on the textiles and ceramics produced for the Ottoman court. The Museum's collection of textiles includes a few examples of the luxury brocades and velvets executed at the early capital of Bursa, renowned from the fifteenth to eighteenth centuries for its fine textiles of floral motifs on backgrounds of red and blue.

Fig. 113
Turkey
Ottoman Period
Ceramic bowl
Iznik, 1550-1600
gift of Harry A. Norton
939.Dp.19

In ceramics, the town of Iznik produced large quantities of tableware for the Ottoman court and tile revetments for the numerous new monuments. The high silica content of the Iznik clay produced a great vitrification of the enamel and a brilliancy of colour greatly admired in Europe. The three stages of development of Iznik pottery consist of a first blue and white period (1490-1525) heavily influenced by Chinese porcelain, followed by a second period known as the "Damascus style" (1525-1550) where the colour scheme is enlarged by the addition of a turquoise blue, pale green and subdued purple, leading to the best known third type, the so called "Rhodes style" produced from 1550 to 1700 and characterized by the use of a raised "tomato-red" glaze. In its varying degrees of excellence this third Iznik type is well represented in the Museum collection by numerous examples. The plate with a floral decor of carnations, tulips, roses, bluebells and green leaves arranged in a balanced composition within a border of Chinese waves (fig. 113) is typical of the period.

In Spain, many of the techniques brought in during Muslim rule remained for several centuries in the country and continued to develop by Muslim artisans working for Christian patrons. Of the Hispano-Arab arts, known as Hispano-Moresque, the art of ceramics reached a degree of excellence and esteem unparalleled in European or Arab production of the time. The technique of lustreware, using metal oxides to achieve a brilliancy akin to that of gold and copper vessels, reached Spain from Iraq and Egypt in the tenth and eleventh centuries. Mastered in Spain, lustreware established Malaga in the fourteenth

century and Manises (in the vicinity of Valencia) in the fifteenth century as world centers for ceramic production. These Hispano-Moresque wares enjoyed such a popularity among the ruling class of Europe that innumerable members of royal and noble families in Spain, France and Italy commissioned lustreware for both table service and decoration and had it emblazoned with their coat of arms. A fine Museum example (fig. 114) is a fifteenth-century plate produced in Manises and carrying the heraldry of the House of Aragon superimposed by that of an unidentified family, on a background of Muslim motifs. Such plates were so carefully executed that the backs as well as the fronts were given considerable attention. The reverse of our plate is decorated with a traditional eagle in bold lines of copper lustre. Next to plates and bowls, albarellos, or

apothecary jars used for the storage of spices and herbs, were abundantly produced during the fifteenth century. The albarello in the Museum's collection shows the traditional shape of a tall concave cylinder with the common motif of blue and yellow leaves of ivy and acacia on a dotted background. Moreover, it carries the rare feature of a glazed label indicating the symbol of its content.

Also in the fifteenth century, tile-mosaics flourished as revetments for architecture. First utilized in palaces, tiles became standard features in all homes, both inside and outside. The examples on display exhibit the major characteristics of the late fifteenth- and early sixteenth-century tiles of brilliant thick glazes in sharply defined outlines to prevent the colours from running. Some motifs like the geometric radiating star shape are purely Arab in nature while others with heraldry and animal motifs betray the influence of Gothic and Renaissance prototypes. Next to ceramics, Hispano-Moresque arts are known by the fine textile production. Numerous examples entered the Museum collection with the purchase of the well-known Arthur Byne collection of Spanish textiles and include fine specimens from the tenth to the seventeenth century representing most techniques and motifs.

The above gives an idea of the richness and variety of Islamic art, both well-represented in the Museum's collection. In spite of the regional developments and local variations of style, Islamic civilization remained a unifying factor over a large and diverse geographic area. The many objects discussed, which were created in various media and at different periods of time, exhibit similar characteristics. They are utilitarian objects with a great concern for a rich surface decoration.

One of the first important acquisitions of pre-Columbian art took place in 1926, when the Philip Means collection of Peruvian textiles came into the possession of the Museum through the efforts of Gordon W. MacDougall, E. I. Barott, Miss Mabel Molson and F. Cleveland Morgan. Today, the Museum houses objects representing many periods of pre-Columbian art.

In the course of pre-Columbian cultural development in the Western Hemisphere, two areas attained heights of civilization unparalleled elsewhere in the New World. These regions, the Andean area and the Mexican-Guatemalan complex, together form what archaeologists call Nuclear America. Until recently, it was believed that satellite cultures spread from these two centers to other areas. However, the excavation of a site belonging to the Valdivia culture of coastal Ecuador would seem to push the beginnings of the Formative stage, defined as that period when there appeared large permanent communities deriving most of their food from farming, back to around 3000 BC. This date is 1000 to

1500 years earlier than the Formative stage was previously thought to have appeared in the Mexican and Peruvian complexes. From Real Alto, the site of the dig, primitive urbanization patterns may have spread toward these centers of later civilizations.

The northern region of development, called Mesoamerica, included, at the time of the Spanish Conquest in 1521, central and southern Mexico with the peninsula of Yucatan, Guatemala, El Salvador, and parts of Honduras, Nicaragua, and northern Costa Rica. This cultural area is divided into two parts — central Mexico, which produced the civilization known as Mexican, and the Maya area, extending from southern Mexico south to the limits of Mesoamerica.

The cultural phases of ancient Mexico are defined as Preclassic or Formative, stretching from 3000 BC to 250 AD; Classic, from 250 AD to 950 AD; and Postclassic, lasting from 950 AD to the time of the Spanish Conquest. During Preclassic and Classic times, the highly gifted Olmec people inhabited the region of southern Veracruz and western Tabasco, side-by-side with a number of lesser peasant groups scattered throughout the area. Olmec sculpture ranges in size from the 8-foot, 15-ton human heads carved of basalt found at La Venta and Tres Zapotes, to small ceramic figures combining human and feline features, such as the one in the

Fig. 115
Mexico
Olmec
1200-400 BC
Baby-face Figure
terracotta with white slip
Veracruz
toward 800 BC
Horsley and Annie Townsend
  Bequest
973.Ac.3

Museum's collection (fig. 115). This "baby face" figurine represents the offspring of a jaguar father and human mother. Seated with legs apart, it lacks any indication of sex or clothing. The artist was nevertheless aware of body structure, depicting it with utmost naturalism. The earlobes are pierced for added ornaments. The jaguar ancestry shows only in the down-drawn corners of the mouth. The horizontal opening at the back of the head is a technically necessary perforation for the escape of moisture and air during the drying and firing of the clay.

The influence of Olmec art penetrated far beyond its geographic boundaries. Regional cultures and styles had been evolving during the Late Preclassic period, incorporating the Olmec elements of simplicity, vigor and realism which spread throughout ancient Mesoamerica from the Gulf Coast. The great city of Teotihuacán, the earliest true urban complex of Mesoamerica, dominated the subsequent Classic period during which expanding population, building activity and trade, along with excellence in the arts, denote an era of well-being and achievement unequaled at any other time. Today, thirteen centuries after its destruction and only 25 miles north of the modern capital of Mexico, Teotihuacán remains the "Place of the Gods", a ruined city covering an area of six square miles dominated by the two gigantic *Pyramids of the Sun and the Moon*. The sculpture of Teotihuacán takes the form of beautifully-worked stone masks, clay or jade statuettes, and cylindrical clay vessels. In fact, the development of the history of the city

Fig. 117
Mexico, Totonac
Classic
100-800 AD
Carved Yoke
stone
purchase
949.50.Ac.1

has been established by the study of its pottery. The Museum's flat-bottomed cylindrical jar (fig. 116) is characteristic of the Teotihuacán III pottery shapes of the flourishing Classic period which ended with the mysterious demise of the city at the end of the seventh century. This ritual vessel, resting on three rectangular feet, probably was covered with a conical lid topped by a handle. The painted decorative motifs, as in the Museum's example, are derived from Maya-inspired mural painting. The principal subjects were the elements of nature, but stylized shapes derived from the headdress, mouth mask and tongue of the rain god, as well as solar symbols and numerals were also used. The lidded cylindrical tripod became Teotihuacán's single most distinguished pot; it has been called the hallmark of the city and was produced in quantity for trade to distant places where rulers valued them as religious paraphenalia as well as luxury imports. Examples have been unearthed as far south as the great Maya city of Copán in Honduras.

The Totonac area of Northern Veracruz has yielded the finest non-architectural stone sculpture in Mesoamerica. The varied and sophisticated work of this school was confined to traditional forms of specialized equipment associated with the ritual ball game, a combination of spectator sport and religious ceremony akin to the bull rites of ancient Crete. A heavy stone yoke (fig. 117) was worn as a belt by the participants in the game. The Museum's late Classic piece is skilfully carved in relief and shows a decided feeling for stylized form. The stylized frog represented on its surface is a reptilian manifestation of the god of the earth. To the Mexican mind, earth and death were ultimately linked. The Museum also possesses a number of wedge-shaped *hachas,* or thin stone heads, used in the ball game ritual.

Fig. 118
Mexico
Classic Maya
200-900 AD
Plate with Two Hunters Holding
    Blowpipes
polychromed terracotta
Horsley and Annie Townsend
    Bequest
968.Ac.5

The Maya area comprises a well-defined zone stretching from southeastern Mexico to Costa Rica. The intellectual scope of the Maya and the complexity of their culture are reflected in the hieroglyphic inscriptions found on commemorative stelae and other stone sculpture, on buildings, on minor works of art and in three manuscripts. These sources record uncanny developments in astronomy, astrology and mathematics which led to the invention of a calendar equal to present-day methods of recording time. The most important period in Maya art is the Classic, from 200 AD to 900 AD, approximately corresponding to the same period in Mexican culture.

In comparison to the solidity, strength and balanced volume of central Mexican art, Maya art seems fluid and graceful. Bright ceramic vessels such as the Museum's terracotta dish from the late Classic period (fig. 118) are important since the spontaneous brushwork is perhaps the principal surviving instance of Maya painting apart from the spectacular frescoes at Bonampak. Despite their complex mentality, the Maya limited their artistic expression to the glorification of the priestly aristocracy and the representation of religious ideas. On a brightly burnished orange background, the artist has depicted hunters wearing high headdresses and short fringed garments with blowguns raised to their lips. Captured birds hang from their belts. The identity of these figures is subject to conjecture: they may represent either priests, or the Maya deity Ek Chuah, the black war captain, or a set of twins described in the *Popol Vuh,* the sacred book of the ancient Quiché Maya.

The entire western side of South America is dominated by the Andes, the most extensive orographic system in the world, sweeping north and south for 4,000 miles. In pre-Columbian times Peru, located in the center of this area, was the home of advanced and organized cultures who built temples, fortresses and irrigation systems. The Chavin of Peru produced works of art that were seldom equaled in later times. Chavin art is bold and voluminous, symmetrically balanced and well made. Its iconography centers around jaguars and elements of jaguars combined with human or bird features. From the Maranon River valley in the north central Andes, Chavin influence spread throughout Peru and, by the mid-first millennium BC, regional distinctions became pronounced. The art of Paracas and later Nazca in the south coast regions, Mohica in the north and Recuay in the central highlands is stylistically as well as regionally distinct.

From an early date, the peoples of the central Andean region had perfected spinning and weaving into a highly skilled technical art. Textiles of extraordinarily fine weave were made on elementary hand looms; the simplicity of his tools did not impede the Peruvian artist from utilizing complex motifs and weave-variants in the production of such imaginative work as the Museum's tapestry panel (fig. 119) from the Nazca culture of approximately 500 AD. The materials used were obtained from the llama, vicuna and alpaca; the sheep was unknown until after the Conquest. Natural vegetable and mineral dyes were processed for colouring, which has survived with remarkable brilliance. On a uniform ground of dark blue, the designer uses small human and animal forms squared to the requirements of the weaving technique. A close inspection of the delicate many-coloured pattern reveals that no two figures are identical. Many wear fringed head-dresses which give a rich texture to the work. Around their necks are yokes ending in animal heads; in their hands some hold serpents and animals. Peruvian fabrics such as the Museum's panel were part of the funerary offerings provided for the dead. The dry climate of the sea coast assured their survival to the present day.

Pre-Columbian art of the Andes, like that of Mexico and Central America, was closely associated with religious beliefs and rituals. Mexican art expresses a dread of supernatural forces, while Peruvian art reveals a civilization at peace with its material and spiritual environment. Mexican art appeals to the viewer's sense of spectacle; Peruvian art bespeaks urbanity and quiet assurance.

Fig. 119
Peru
Nazca
100 BC — 600 AD
Tapestry-weave Panel
wool and cotton
gift of F. Cleveland Morgan
948.Ad.35

Graphic design:	Jacques Guillon/Designers Inc.
Printing:	Laplante + Langevin Inc.
Typesetting:	Compoplus Typesetters Inc.
Additional Photography:	A. Kilbertus
Secretariat:	Marilyn Aitken Liliane Asselin Deborah Brockman Georgette Calinesco Christiane M. Schelhot Louise Vachon

Paper
Cover:	Regent coated litho
Interior pages:	Cameo dull ● 80 lbs.
Number printed:	5,000 copies
Publication:	1977